STARTING A FOOD TRUCK BUSINESS

Four Wheels, Endless Flavors: The Guerrilla Guide to Building a Thriving Yummy Empire, From Curbside to Culinary Star

Arthur D. Garcia

Copyright © 2024 by Arthur D. Garcia

All rights reserved. No part of this book may be reproduced, distributed, or transmitted in any form or by any means, including photocopying, recording, or other electronic or mechanical methods, without the prior written permission of the publisher, except in the case of brief quotations embodied in critical reviews and specific other noncommercial uses permitted by copyright law

TABLE OF CONTENTS
  1

CHAPTER 1:   6
INTRODUCTION TO THE FOOD TRUCK INDUSTRY   6
    1.1 UNDERSTANDING THE FOOD TRUCK PHENOMENON   11
    1.2 ADVANTAGES OF STARTING A FOOD TRUCK BUSINESS   15
    1.3 Challenges and Considerations   19
    1.4 MARKET ANALYSIS AND RESEARCH   23

CHAPTER 2:   27
CRAFTING YOUR FOOD TRUCK CONCEPT   27
    2.1 IDENTIFYING YOUR NICHE   31
    2.2 DEVELOPING YOUR MENU   35
    2.3 FOOD SAFETY AND REGULATIONS   40
    2.4 DESIGNING YOUR FOOD TRUCK   44

CHAPTER 3:   49
BUSINESS PLANNING AND FINANCIAL MANAGEMENT   49
    3.1 WRITING A BUSINESS PLAN   54
    3.2 BUDGETING AND FINANCIAL FORECASTING   60
    3.3 FUNDING YOUR FOOD TRUCK VENTURE   65
    3.4 PRICING STRATEGY AND REVENUE MODELS   69

CHAPTER 4:   73
LEGAL AND REGULATORY CONSIDERATIONS   73
    4.1 LICENSING AND PERMITS   79
    4.2 HEALTH AND SAFETY REGULATIONS   83
    4.3 INSURANCE FOR FOOD TRUCKS   87
    4.4 TAXATION AND BUSINESS STRUCTURE   92

CHAPTER 5: **97**
SOURCING INGREDIENTS AND SUPPLIERS **97**
   5.1 BUILDING RELATIONSHIPS WITH SUPPLIERS 102
   5.2 ENSURING QUALITY AND CONSISTENCY 107
   5.3 SUSTAINABLE SOURCING PRACTICES 111
   5.4 MANAGING INVENTORY 116

CHAPTER 6: **121**
MARKETING AND BRANDING STRATEGIES **121**
   6.1 CREATING A STRONG BRAND IDENTITY 126
   6.2 BUILDING AN ONLINE PRESENCE 130
   6.3 SOCIAL MEDIA MARKETING TACTICS 135
   6.4 EVENT MARKETING AND COLLABORATIONS 141

CHAPTER 7: **147**
OPERATIONS AND LOGISTICS **147**
   7.1 PLANNING YOUR ROUTE AND SCHEDULE 153
   7.2 MANAGING STAFF AND TRAINING 158
   7.3 EQUIPMENT MAINTENANCE AND UPKEEP 164
   7.4 STREAMLINING OPERATIONS FOR EFFICIENCY 170

CHAPTER 8: **176**
GROWTH AND EXPANSION OPPORTUNITIES **176**
   8.1 SCALING YOUR FOOD TRUCK BUSINESS 181
   8.2 DIVERSIFYING REVENUE STREAMS 186
   8.3 FRANCHISING OR LICENSING YOUR CONCEPT 192
   8.4 EXPLORING BRICK-AND-MORTAR OPTIONS 198

CONCLUSION **205**

CHAPTER 1:
INTRODUCTION TO THE FOOD TRUCK INDUSTRY

In recent years, the food truck industry has exploded onto the culinary scene, offering a diverse array of delicious and convenient dining options. Whether you're craving tacos, burgers, or gourmet cupcakes, there's likely a food truck serving up exactly what you're looking for just around the corner. But what exactly is the food truck industry, and what makes it such an appealing venture for entrepreneurs? In this chapter, we'll explore the ins and outs of the food truck industry, from its humble beginnings to its current status as a thriving business sector.

The Rise of Food Trucks

The concept of selling food from a mobile vehicle dates back centuries, but it wasn't until the early 2000s that food trucks experienced a resurgence in popularity. Fuelled by a combination of economic factors, changing consumer preferences, and advancements in technology, food trucks began popping up in cities across the globe, offering a convenient and affordable alternative to traditional brick-and-mortar restaurants.

Personal Experience:
As a budding entrepreneur with a passion for cooking, I found myself drawn to the idea of starting my own food truck business. Inspired by the vibrant street food scenes I encountered while traveling, I saw an opportunity to bring unique and delicious cuisine to my local community. Armed with a love for food and a drive to succeed, I set out to learn everything I could about the food truck industry and what it takes to thrive in this competitive market.

Why Start a Food Truck Business?

There are many reasons why aspiring entrepreneurs are drawn to the food truck industry. For starters, the relatively low startup costs make it an attractive option for those looking to break into the restaurant business without breaking the bank. Unlike traditional restaurants, which require significant investments in real estate, renovations, and furnishings, food trucks can be launched with just a fraction of the capital.

Personal Experience:
When I began researching the costs associated with starting a food truck business, I was pleasantly surprised by how affordable it could be. Instead of shelling out thousands of dollars for a storefront lease and renovations, I could invest in a used food truck, outfit it with the necessary equipment, and hit

the road in a matter of weeks. This low barrier to entry made the prospect of starting my own business seem not only feasible but downright exciting.

In addition to lower startup costs, food trucks also offer flexibility and mobility that traditional restaurants can't match.

Rather than being tied to a single location, food truck owners have the freedom to roam the streets, catering to different neighborhoods, events, and festivals throughout the week. This flexibility not only allows for greater exposure and reach but also enables entrepreneurs to adapt to changing market conditions and customer preferences on the fly.

Personal Experience:
One of the things that appealed to me most about the food truck industry was the opportunity to take my culinary creations directly to my customers. Instead of waiting for diners to come to me, I could bring my food to them, setting up shop at farmers' markets, office parks, and special events. This direct interaction not only allowed me to build a loyal customer base but also provided valuable feedback and insights that helped me refine my menu and offerings over time.

Despite its many advantages, the food truck industry is not without its challenges.

From navigating complex regulations and permits to dealing with unpredictable weather and competition, food truck owners face a unique set of hurdles on their path to success. However, with careful planning, perseverance, and a dash of creativity, many entrepreneurs have found that the rewards far outweigh the risks.

Personal Experience:
Launching my food truck business was not without its challenges, but every obstacle I encountered only strengthened my resolve to succeed. From securing the necessary permits and licenses to fine-tuning my menu and marketing strategy, there were countless hurdles to overcome along the way. However, with each setback came a valuable lesson, and I soon learned that resilience and determination were just as important as culinary skill when it came to running a successful food truck business.

In the following chapters, we'll dive deeper into the various aspects of starting and running a food truck business, from crafting a winning menu to navigating the legal and regulatory landscape. Whether you're a seasoned chef looking to strike out on your own or a budding entrepreneur with a passion for food, the food truck industry offers an exciting and wonderful chance to realize your goals of becoming a chef. So, grab your apron and join me as we embark on this delicious journey together!

1.1 UNDERSTANDING THE FOOD TRUCK PHENOMENON

The food truck phenomenon has taken the culinary world by storm, transforming the way we eat and experience food. But what exactly is it about food trucks that has captured the hearts and taste buds of people around the world? In this section, we'll delve into the key factors driving the popularity of food trucks and explore why they've become such a ubiquitous presence in cities big and small.

Accessibility and Convenience

One of the primary appeals of food trucks is their accessibility and convenience. Unlike traditional restaurants, which are often located in fixed locations and require diners to sit down for a meal, food trucks bring the dining experience directly to the customer. Whether you're grabbing a quick bite on your lunch break or sampling street food at a local festival, food trucks offer a convenient and hassle-free way to satisfy your hunger on the go.

Variety and Innovation

Another reason for the popularity of food trucks is the wide variety of culinary offerings they provide. From classic comfort foods like burgers and fries to exotic cuisines from around the world, food trucks cater to a diverse range of tastes and preferences. What's more, many food truck chefs pride themselves on their ability to innovate and experiment with unique flavor combinations and cooking techniques, offering customers a one-of-a-kind dining experience they won't find anywhere else.

Affordability and Value

In addition to their accessibility and variety, food trucks are also known for offering affordable and value-packed meals. With lower overhead costs compared to traditional restaurants, food truck owners are able to pass on savings to their customers in the form of lower prices and generous portion sizes. This makes food trucks an attractive option for budget-conscious diners looking to enjoy a delicious meal without breaking the bank.

Social and Cultural Experience

Food trucks also offer a social and cultural experience that extends beyond just eating. Whether you're waiting in line for your favorite food truck or striking up a conversation with fellow diners at a communal table, food trucks have a way of bringing people together and fostering a sense of community. In addition, many food truck events and festivals feature live music, entertainment, and other attractions, turning a simple meal into a memorable and enjoyable outing for friends and family alike.

Adaptability and Resilience

One of the most remarkable aspects of the food truck phenomenon is its adaptability and resilience in the face of adversity. From economic downturns to public health crises, food trucks have proven to be remarkably resilient businesses, able to pivot and innovate to meet the changing needs and preferences of their customers. Whether it's offering contactless ordering and delivery or partnering with local farmers and suppliers to source fresh, seasonal ingredients, food trucks have demonstrated an impressive ability to adapt and thrive in an ever-changing landscape.

Conclusion

In conclusion, the food truck phenomenon is a testament to the power of innovation, creativity, and community in the culinary world. With their accessibility, variety, affordability, and social appeal, food trucks have captured the imagination of food lovers everywhere, redefining the way we eat and experience food on a daily basis. Whether you're a seasoned foodie or simply looking for a delicious and convenient meal on the go, food trucks offer something for everyone, making them a beloved and enduring fixture of city streets and neighborhoods around the world.

1.2 ADVANTAGES OF STARTING A FOOD TRUCK BUSINESS

Starting a food truck business offers a unique set of advantages that make it an appealing venture for entrepreneurs looking to break into the culinary industry. In this section, we'll explore some of the key benefits of launching your own food truck and why it might be the perfect opportunity for you to turn your passion for food into a profitable business.

Lower Startup Costs

One of the biggest advantages of starting a food truck business is the lower startup costs compared to traditional brick-and-mortar restaurants. Unlike restaurants, which require significant investments in real estate, renovations, and furnishings, food trucks can be launched with just a fraction of the capital. By purchasing a used food truck and outfitting it with the necessary equipment, aspiring food truck owners can significantly reduce their upfront expenses, making entrepreneurship more accessible and achievable.

Flexible Location and Hours

Another advantage of starting a food truck business is the flexibility it offers in terms of location and operating hours. Unlike fixed-location restaurants, which are tied to a single location and operating hours, food trucks have the freedom to roam the streets, catering to different neighborhoods, events, and festivals throughout the week. This flexibility not only allows for greater exposure and reach but also enables entrepreneurs to adapt to changing market conditions and customer preferences on the fly.

Lower Overhead Costs

In addition to lower startup costs, food truck businesses also benefit from lower ongoing overhead costs compared to traditional restaurants. With no rent or property taxes to worry about, food truck owners can allocate more of their revenue towards ingredients, equipment maintenance, and marketing efforts, helping to maximize profitability and sustainability in the long run. This lean operating model allows food truck businesses to weather economic downturns and fluctuations in consumer spending more effectively than their brick-and-mortar counterparts.

Direct Customer Interaction

One of the most rewarding aspects of starting a food truck business is the opportunity for direct customer interaction. Unlike chefs and restaurant owners who are often hidden away in the kitchen, food truck owners have the chance to interact with their customers face-to-face, building personal connections and fostering a sense of community and loyalty. Whether it's chatting with diners about their favorite menu items or receiving real-time feedback on new dishes, the direct customer interaction that food trucks offer can be incredibly valuable in shaping the success and direction of the business.

Creative Freedom and Innovation

Food trucks also offer entrepreneurs a platform for creative freedom and innovation in the culinary world. With no fixed menu or set cuisine, food truck owners have the freedom to experiment with different flavors, ingredients, and cooking techniques, constantly pushing the boundaries of traditional cuisine and offering customers a truly unique and memorable dining experience. Whether it's fusion tacos, gourmet grilled cheese sandwiches, or artisanal ice cream, food trucks have become synonymous with culinary creativity and innovation, attracting food lovers of all tastes and preferences.

Conclusion

In conclusion, starting a food truck business offers a multitude of advantages that make it an attractive venture for aspiring entrepreneurs in the culinary industry. From lower startup costs and flexible operating hours to direct customer interaction and creative freedom, food trucks provide a unique opportunity to turn your passion for food into a profitable and rewarding business. Whether you're a seasoned chef looking to strike out on your own or a budding entrepreneur with a love for food, the advantages of starting a food truck business are clear: it's a deliciously exciting opportunity with the potential for success and satisfaction in equal measure.

1.3 Challenges and Considerations

While starting a food truck business offers many advantages, it's essential to be aware of the challenges and considerations that come with the territory. In this section, we'll explore some of the key challenges that aspiring food truck owners may face and provide insights into how to overcome them effectively.

Regulatory and Permitting Requirements

One of the most significant challenges of starting a food truck business is navigating the complex web of regulatory and permitting requirements. Depending on your location, you may need to obtain various permits and licenses to operate legally, including health department permits, business licenses, and zoning approvals. Understanding and complying with these requirements can be time-consuming and costly, but it's essential to ensure that you're operating within the law and protecting the health and safety of your customers.

Financial Planning and Budgeting

Another challenge of starting a food truck business is financial planning and budgeting. While food trucks generally have lower startup costs than traditional restaurants, they still require a significant investment in equipment, supplies, and marketing efforts. It's crucial to create a detailed business plan that outlines your startup costs, operating expenses, and revenue projections to ensure that you have a clear understanding of your finances and are able to make well-informed business decisions.

Competition and Market Saturation

As the popularity of food trucks continues to grow, so too does the level of competition in the industry. In many cities, the market may already be saturated with established food truck operators, making it challenging for newcomers to carve out a niche and attract customers. It's essential to conduct thorough market research to identify gaps in the market and differentiate your food truck from the competition, whether through unique menu offerings, innovative marketing strategies, or exceptional customer service.

Seasonality and Weather

Seasonality and weather can also pose significant challenges for food truck owners, particularly in regions with extreme climates. Inclement weather, such as rain, snow, or excessive heat, can impact customer turnout and sales, making it difficult to maintain a consistent revenue stream. It's essential to have a contingency plan in place for adverse weather conditions, whether it's investing in a weatherproof canopy, diversifying your revenue streams through catering or events, or temporarily closing during inclement weather.

Equipment Maintenance and Repairs

Keeping your food truck in good working order is essential for maintaining the quality and consistency of your food and ensuring the safety of your customers. However, equipment maintenance and repairs can be costly and time-consuming, particularly if you're dealing with unexpected breakdowns or malfunctions. It's crucial to invest in high-quality equipment and establish a regular maintenance schedule to prevent issues before they arise. Additionally, having a contingency fund set aside for unexpected repairs can help mitigate the financial impact of equipment failures.

Work-Life Balance

Running a food truck business can be demanding and time-consuming, often requiring long hours and weekends spent on the road. Maintaining a healthy work-life balance can be challenging, particularly for entrepreneurs who are passionate about their business and eager to succeed. It's essential to prioritize self-care and set boundaries to prevent burnout, whether it's scheduling regular breaks, delegating tasks to trusted staff members, or taking time off to recharge and rejuvenate.

Conclusion

While starting a food truck business offers many opportunities for success and fulfillment, it's essential to be aware of the challenges and considerations that come with the territory. From navigating regulatory requirements and financial planning to managing competition and maintaining work-life balance, there are many factors to consider when launching and operating a food truck business. However, with careful planning, perseverance, and a willingness to adapt, many aspiring food truck owners have found that the rewards far outweigh the challenges, making it a deliciously exciting venture worth pursuing.

1.4 MARKET ANALYSIS AND RESEARCH

Before launching a food truck business, conducting thorough market analysis and research is essential to understand the demand, competition, and potential opportunities in your target market. In this section, we'll explore the key steps involved in market analysis and research and provide insights into how to gather and interpret the data effectively.

Identifying Your Target Market

The first step in market analysis is to identify your target market – the specific demographic or group of people who are most likely to patronize your food truck. This may include factors such as age, gender, income level, lifestyle preferences, and dietary restrictions. By understanding your target market's needs, preferences, and purchasing behavior, you can tailor your menu, marketing efforts, and overall business strategy to effectively appeal to and attract customers.

Conducting Competitor Analysis

Once you've identified your target market, the next step is to conduct a competitor analysis to assess the competitive landscape in your area. This involves researching and evaluating other food trucks and restaurants that offer similar cuisine or cater to a similar demographic. Key factors to consider include their menu offerings, pricing strategies, customer reviews, branding and marketing efforts, and overall market share. By understanding your competitors' strengths and weaknesses, you can identify opportunities to differentiate your food truck and carve out a unique position in the market.

Assessing Market Demand

Assessing market demand is another crucial aspect of market analysis, as it helps determine the potential profitability and viability of your food truck business. This involves researching and analyzing factors such as population demographics, consumer trends, economic indicators, and local events and festivals that may impact demand for your products. By understanding the current and projected demand for your cuisine in your target market, you can make informed decisions about menu development, pricing strategies, and location selection to maximize your chances of success.

Gathering Customer Feedback

In addition to conducting market research, gathering customer feedback is an invaluable tool for gaining insights into your target market's preferences and preferences. This can be done through various methods, including surveys, focus groups, social media engagement, and direct interactions with customers at food truck events and festivals. By soliciting feedback from your target market, you can identify areas for improvement, refine your menu offerings, and tailor your marketing efforts to better meet the needs and desires of your customers.

Analyzing Regulatory and Permitting Requirements

Finally, as part of your market analysis, it's essential to research and analyze the regulatory and permitting requirements for operating a food truck in your area. This may include obtaining health department permits, business licenses, zoning approvals, and parking permits, among others. Understanding and complying with these requirements is critical to ensuring that your food truck operates legally and safely, and can help prevent costly fines, penalties, and legal issues down the line.

Conclusion

In conclusion, market analysis and research are essential steps in the process of starting a food truck business. By identifying your target market, conducting competitor analysis, assessing market demand, gathering customer feedback, and analyzing regulatory requirements, you can gain valuable insights into the opportunities and challenges that exist in your target market. Armed with this information, you can develop a strategic business plan, make informed decisions, and position your food truck for success in the competitive culinary landscape.

CHAPTER 2:

CRAFTING YOUR FOOD TRUCK CONCEPT

Crafting your food truck concept is an exciting and crucial step in starting a successful food truck business. In this chapter, we'll explore the key elements involved in developing your food truck concept, from identifying your niche to designing your menu and branding. Drawing from personal experiences and industry insights, we'll provide actionable tips and strategies to help you create a compelling and profitable food truck concept that resonates with your target audience.

Identifying Your Niche

The first step in crafting your food truck concept is to identify your niche – the specific cuisine, theme, or culinary style that sets your food truck apart from the competition. Consider your personal background, interests, and expertise, as well as market demand and trends, when choosing your niche. Whether it's gourmet burgers, authentic tacos, or vegan comfort food, selecting a niche that aligns with your passion and expertise can help differentiate your food truck and attract a loyal customer base.

Personal Experience:
When I was brainstorming ideas for my food truck concept, I drew inspiration from my travels and culinary experiences. Having spent years exploring different cuisines and cooking techniques, I decided to focus on fusion street food – a unique blend of global flavors and local ingredients that reflects my love for experimentation and creativity. By carving out a niche in the crowded food truck market, I was able to stand out from the competition and attract customers who were eager to try something new and exciting.

Developing Your Menu

Once you've identified your niche, the next step is to develop your menu – the assortment of dishes and offerings that will be the cornerstone of your food truck concept. Keep your target audience in mind when designing your menu, and strive to strike a balance between familiar favorites and innovative creations. Consider factors such as ingredient availability, food cost, and preparation time when selecting menu items, and aim to create a diverse and balanced selection that appeals to a wide range of tastes and preferences.

Personal Experience:

When designing my food truck menu, I focused on creating a curated selection of signature dishes that showcased the unique flavors and ingredients of my fusion street food concept. Drawing inspiration from my favorite international cuisines, I developed a menu that featured bold and flavorful dishes like Korean BBQ tacos, Thai-inspired noodle bowls, and Mexican street corn with a twist. By offering a diverse range of options that catered to both meat lovers and vegetarians alike, I was able to attract a broad customer base and keep them coming back for more.

Creating Your Brand Identity

In addition to your menu, your food truck concept should also encompass your brand identity – the visual and emotional elements that define your business and set it apart from the competition. Consider factors such as your food truck's name, logo, color scheme, and overall aesthetic when crafting your brand identity, and strive to create a cohesive and memorable brand that resonates with your target audience. Your brand identity should reflect the unique personality and values of your food truck concept, and evoke a positive emotional response from customers.

Personal Experience:
When it came to creating my food truck's brand identity, I wanted to capture the spirit of adventure and exploration that inspired my fusion street food concept. I chose a name that reflected this ethos – "Global Bites" – and designed a logo that combined bold typography with playful graphics and vibrant colors. From the moment customers saw my food truck on the street, I wanted them to feel a sense of excitement and curiosity about what culinary adventures awaited them inside. By staying true to my brand identity and consistently reinforcing it through my food, service, and marketing efforts, I was able to build a strong and recognizable brand that struck a chord with clients and aided in business expansion.

Conclusion

Crafting your food truck concept is a multifaceted process that requires careful consideration and planning. By identifying your niche, developing a standout menu, and creating a compelling brand identity, you can create a food truck concept that captivates customers and sets you up for success in the competitive culinary landscape. Drawing from personal experiences and industry insights, you can create a food truck concept that not only delights customers but also fulfills your passion for food and entrepreneurship.

2.1 IDENTIFYING YOUR NICHE

Identifying your niche is a critical step in crafting a successful food truck concept. Your niche is what sets you apart from the competition and defines the unique value proposition of your food truck. In this section, we'll explore the key considerations and strategies involved in identifying your niche, drawing from personal experiences and industry insights to help you find the perfect fit for your food truck concept.

Understand Your Passion and Expertise

The first step in identifying your niche is to understand your passion and expertise in the culinary world. Consider your background, training, and culinary experiences, as well as your personal preferences and interests. Which culinary arts do you excel in? What dishes do you enjoy cooking the most? By identifying your strengths and areas of expertise, you can narrow down your options and focus on developing a niche that aligns with your skills and interests.

Personal Experience:
When I was first exploring the idea of starting a food truck business, I reflected on my own culinary journey and the dishes that I felt most passionate about. As someone who had spent years experimenting with different cuisines and cooking techniques, I realized that my true passion lay in fusion cuisine – the art of blending flavors and ingredients from diverse culinary traditions to create bold and exciting dishes. Drawing inspiration from my travels and culinary adventures, I decided to make fusion street food the focus of my food truck concept.

Research Market Demand and Trends

In addition to understanding your own passion and expertise, it's essential to research market demand and trends in the food truck industry. Look for gaps in the market where there may be unmet demand or underserved customer segments. Pay attention to emerging culinary trends and consumer preferences, such as plant-based cuisine, artisanal street food, or regional specialties. By identifying areas of opportunity and aligning your niche with current market trends, you can position your food truck for success in the competitive culinary landscape.

Personal Experience:

As I delved deeper into my research, I discovered a growing trend towards global flavors and international street food. People were increasingly seeking out unique and adventurous dining experiences, driven by a desire to explore new cultures and cuisines. Recognizing this trend, I saw an opportunity to carve out a niche for myself by offering fusion street food that combined the best elements of different culinary traditions into one exciting and delicious package. By aligning my niche with market demand and trends, I felt confident that I could create a food truck concept that would resonate with customers and stand out in the crowded marketplace.

Consider Your Target Audience

Another important factor to consider when identifying your niche is your target audience – the specific demographic or group of people you'll be catering to with your food truck concept. Consider factors such as age, gender, income level, lifestyle preferences, and dietary restrictions when defining your target audience. What types of cuisine are they most interested in? What flavor profiles and ingredients do they prefer? By understanding your target audience's needs and preferences, you can tailor your niche to better meet their expectations and attract their patronage.

Personal Experience:
In my case, I identified my target audience as adventurous food lovers who were eager to explore new flavors and culinary experiences. These were people who appreciated bold and inventive dishes that pushed the boundaries of traditional cuisine. Armed with this knowledge, I knew that my fusion street food concept would resonate with them, offering a unique and exciting alternative to more conventional dining options. By keeping my target audience in mind throughout the development of my niche, I was able to create a food truck concept that spoke directly to their tastes and preferences.

Conclusion

Identifying your niche is a crucial step in crafting a successful food truck concept. By understanding your passion and expertise, researching market demand and trends, and considering your target audience, you can pinpoint the perfect niche for your food truck and create a strong value proposition that distinguishes you from the competitors. Drawing from personal experiences and industry insights, you can develop a niche that not only resonates with customers but also fulfills your passion for food and entrepreneurship.

2.2 DEVELOPING YOUR MENU

Developing your menu is a crucial aspect of crafting a successful food truck concept. Your menu is not only a reflection of your culinary skills and creativity but also a key factor in attracting and retaining customers. In this section, we'll explore the step-by-step process of developing a menu for your food truck, drawing from personal experiences and industry insights to help you create a compelling and profitable menu that sets your food truck apart from the competition.

1. Define Your Concept and Cuisine

The first step in developing your menu is to define your concept and cuisine. Consider the niche you identified in the previous section and the unique value proposition of your food truck. What types of dishes and flavors align with your concept? What culinary traditions or styles will you draw inspiration from? By defining your concept and cuisine upfront, you can establish a clear direction for your menu and ensure that all of your offerings are cohesive and consistent.

2. Research and Brainstorm Menu Ideas

Once you've defined your concept and cuisine, it's time to research and brainstorm menu ideas. Look for inspiration from a variety of sources, including cookbooks, culinary magazines, restaurant menus, and food blogs. Consider both classic favorites and innovative creations that showcase your unique twist on familiar dishes. Brainstorm a wide range of menu ideas, from appetizers and entrees to sides and desserts, and experiment with different flavor combinations and ingredient pairings to find the perfect balance for your menu.

3. Consider Seasonality and Regional Ingredients

When developing your menu, it's essential to consider seasonality and the availability of regional ingredients. Choose ingredients that are fresh, seasonal, and locally sourced whenever possible, as these will not only be more flavorful but also more cost-effective. Incorporate seasonal specials and limited-time offerings to keep your menu fresh and exciting throughout the year, and highlight the unique flavors and ingredients of your region to add an authentic touch to your cuisine.

4. Balance Variety and Cohesion

A successful menu strikes a balance between variety and cohesion, offering enough diversity to appeal to a wide range of tastes and preferences while maintaining a cohesive theme and style. Aim to include a mix of familiar favorites and signature dishes that showcase your culinary expertise and creativity. Consider offering options for different dietary preferences, such as vegetarian, vegan, and gluten-free dishes, to ensure that all of your customers can find something they love on your menu.

5. Price Strategically

When pricing your menu items, it's essential to strike a balance between profitability and affordability. Consider factors such as ingredient costs, preparation time, and market demand when determining your prices, and aim to offer competitive pricing that reflects the value of your dishes. Avoid pricing yourself out of the market by setting prices too high, but also be wary of underpricing your offerings and undercutting your profitability. Experiment with pricing strategies, such as bundle deals or combo meals, to maximize sales and encourage upselling.

6. Test and Refine

Once you've finalized your menu, it's time to test and refine your dishes to ensure that they meet your quality and flavor standards. Conduct taste tests with friends, family, and potential customers to gather feedback and identify any areas for improvement. Pay attention to factors such as portion sizes, seasoning, texture, and presentation, and be open to making adjustments based on feedback. Continuously monitor customer feedback and sales data to identify popular dishes and trends, and be willing to make changes to your menu as needed to keep it fresh and relevant.

7. Create Eye-Catching Descriptions and Imagery

In addition to the dishes themselves, it's essential to create eye-catching descriptions and imagery for your menu items. Use descriptive language that highlights the flavors, ingredients, and unique selling points of each dish, and consider incorporating mouth-watering photos or illustrations to entice customers. Invest in professional menu design and printing to ensure that your menu is visually appealing and easy to read, and consider incorporating branding elements such as your logo and color scheme to reinforce your brand identity.

Conclusion

Developing your menu is a creative and iterative process that requires careful planning, experimentation, and attention to detail. By defining your concept and cuisine, researching menu ideas, considering seasonality and regional ingredients, balancing variety and cohesion, pricing strategically, testing and refining your dishes, and creating eye-catching descriptions and imagery, you can create a compelling and profitable menu that sets your food truck apart from the competition. Drawing from personal experiences and industry insights, you can develop a menu that not only delights customers but also fulfills your passion for food and entrepreneurship.

2.3 FOOD SAFETY AND REGULATIONS

Ensuring food safety is paramount in the food truck industry to protect the health and well-being of customers and maintain regulatory compliance. In this section, we'll explore the key food safety practices and regulations that food truck owners need to adhere to, providing actionable insights to help you run a safe and successful food truck operation.

Understanding Food Safety Principles

Food safety encompasses a range of practices aimed at preventing foodborne illness and contamination. Some essential food safety principles include proper handwashing, maintaining clean and sanitized food preparation surfaces and equipment, storing food at safe temperatures, preventing cross-contamination between raw and cooked foods, and ensuring proper cooking and reheating temperatures. By understanding and implementing these principles, you can minimize the risk of foodborne illness and ensure the safety of your customers.

Personal Experience:
When I first started my food truck business, I made it a priority to familiarize myself with food safety

principles and regulations. I underwent food safety training and certification to ensure that I had the knowledge and skills necessary to maintain a safe and hygienic food truck operation. I implemented strict protocols for handwashing, cleaning, and sanitizing, and invested in equipment such as thermometers and refrigeration units to monitor and maintain safe food temperatures. By prioritizing food safety from the outset, I was able to build trust and confidence with my customers and maintain a strong reputation for quality and cleanliness.

Complying with Regulatory Requirements

In addition to following food safety best practices, food truck owners must also comply with regulatory requirements set forth by local health departments and governing agencies. These regulations may vary depending on your location but often include obtaining permits and licenses, undergoing inspections, and adhering to specific food handling and storage guidelines. It's essential to familiarize yourself with the regulatory requirements in your area and ensure that your food truck operation meets all necessary standards to avoid fines, penalties, and legal issues.

Personal Experience:
Navigating regulatory requirements can be daunting, but it's a necessary part of running a food truck

business. When I first started my food truck, I reached out to my local health department to inquire about the necessary permits and licenses required to operate legally. I worked closely with health department officials to ensure that my food truck met all regulatory standards for food safety and sanitation, including proper handwashing facilities, food storage practices, and waste disposal procedures. By proactively addressing regulatory requirements, I was able to obtain the necessary permits and launch my food truck operation with confidence.

Implementing Food Safety Protocols

To maintain food safety in your food truck operation, it's essential to establish and implement robust food safety protocols and procedures. This includes developing a written food safety plan that outlines specific practices and protocols for food handling, preparation, storage, and service. Train your staff on proper food safety practices and procedures, including handwashing, sanitizing, and temperature control, and regularly review and reinforce these protocols to ensure compliance and consistency.

Personal Experience:
As my food truck business grew, I hired additional staff to help me manage day-to-day operations. I made it a priority to train my staff on food safety

practices and protocols, emphasizing the importance of proper handwashing, cleaning, and sanitizing at all times. I developed a detailed food safety plan that outlined specific procedures for handling and storing food, monitoring temperatures, and preventing cross-contamination, and conducted regular training sessions to ensure that all staff members were familiar with and adhering to these protocols. By instilling a culture of food safety within my team, I was able to maintain high standards of cleanliness and hygiene throughout my food truck operation.

Conclusion

Food safety is a fundamental aspect of running a successful food truck business. By understanding food safety principles, complying with regulatory requirements, implementing robust food safety protocols, and training your staff effectively, you can ensure the safety and well-being of your customers and protect the reputation and viability of your food truck operation. Drawing from personal experiences and industry insights, you can create a safe and hygienic environment that instills trust and confidence with your customers and sets your food truck apart as a leader in food safety excellence.

2.4 DESIGNING YOUR FOOD TRUCK

Designing your food truck is an exciting and important aspect of creating a successful mobile culinary business. In this section, we'll explore the key considerations and steps involved in designing your food truck, from selecting the right vehicle to creating a functional and eye-catching layout that maximizes efficiency and customer appeal.

Choosing the Right Vehicle

The first step in designing your food truck is selecting the right vehicle to serve as the foundation for your mobile kitchen. Consider factors such as size, layout, and condition when choosing your food truck, and opt for a vehicle that meets your specific needs and budget. Whether you're starting with a new custom-built truck or retrofitting an existing vehicle, it's essential to ensure that your food truck provides ample space for food preparation, storage, and service, as well as compliance with local health and safety regulations.

Personal Experience:
When I was designing my food truck, I opted for a used step van that had been previously used for delivery purposes. I chose this vehicle for its spacious interior and reliable mechanical condition,

as well as its affordability compared to new custom-built trucks. While the initial investment was lower, I made sure to thoroughly inspect the vehicle and address any maintenance issues before outfitting it for my food truck business. By starting with a solid foundation, I was able to create a functional and efficient mobile kitchen that met my needs and exceeded my expectations.

Creating a Functional Layout

Once you've selected your vehicle, the next step is to create a functional layout for your food truck interior. Consider the flow of traffic and operations within the truck, and design a layout that maximizes efficiency and minimizes bottlenecks. Divide the interior space into distinct zones for food preparation, cooking, storage, and service, and ensure that each area is equipped with the necessary equipment and supplies to support its function. Optimize the layout to minimize unnecessary movement and optimize workflow, allowing your team to work seamlessly and efficiently during busy service periods.

Personal Experience:
When designing the layout for my food truck, I consulted with a professional kitchen designer to ensure that every inch of space was utilized effectively. I divided the interior into separate zones

for food preparation, cooking, and service, with designated areas for storage and washing up. I installed custom-built stainless steel countertops and shelving units to maximize workspace and storage capacity, and invested in high-quality equipment such as grills, fryers, and refrigeration units to support my menu offerings. By carefully planning the layout, I was able to create a functional and ergonomic kitchen that allowed my team to work efficiently and deliver top-quality food to our customers.

Incorporating Branding and Signage

In addition to the interior layout, it's essential to incorporate branding and signage into your food truck design to create a strong visual identity and attract customers. Choose a memorable and eye-catching name for your food truck, and design a logo and color scheme that reflect your brand's personality and values. Incorporate branding elements into your exterior signage, menu boards, and vehicle wrap to create a cohesive and professional look that stands out on the street and captures the attention of passersby.

Personal Experience:
Branding was a key consideration in the design of my food truck, as I wanted to create a strong visual identity that would resonate with customers and set

my business apart from the competition. I worked with a graphic designer to develop a logo and color scheme that reflected the adventurous and eclectic nature of my fusion street food concept, and incorporated these elements into the design of my exterior signage and vehicle wrap. The result was a bold and eye-catching food truck that attracted attention wherever it went, helping to drive foot traffic and build brand awareness in the community.

Ensuring Compliance with Health and Safety Regulations

Finally, it's essential to ensure that your food truck design complies with health and safety regulations set forth by local authorities. This may include requirements for equipment installation, ventilation, fire suppression systems, and sanitation facilities, among others. Work with a qualified contractor or consultant to ensure that your food truck meets all necessary standards and regulations, and obtain any required permits or certifications before launching your operation.

Personal Experience:
Compliance with health and safety regulations was a top priority for me when designing my food truck, as I wanted to ensure that my business operated legally and responsibly. I worked closely with health department officials and regulatory agencies to

ensure that my food truck met all necessary requirements for equipment installation, ventilation, and sanitation facilities. I invested in a commercial-grade ventilation system and fire suppression system to ensure the safety of my staff and customers, and obtained all required permits and certifications before launching my operation. By prioritizing compliance from the outset, I was able to operate my food truck with confidence and peace of mind, knowing that I was providing a safe and hygienic dining experience for my customers.

Conclusion

Designing your food truck is a multifaceted process that requires careful planning, creativity, and attention to detail. By choosing the right vehicle, creating a functional layout, incorporating branding and signage, and ensuring compliance with health and safety regulations, you can create a food truck that not only looks great but also operates efficiently and safely. Drawing from personal experiences and industry insights, you can design a food truck that reflects your brand's personality and values, captures the attention of customers, and sets you up for success in the competitive mobile culinary landscape.

CHAPTER 3:

BUSINESS PLANNING AND FINANCIAL MANAGEMENT

In this chapter, we'll delve into the essential aspects of business planning and financial management for your food truck venture. From creating a comprehensive business plan to managing your finances effectively, we'll explore the key steps and strategies to help you build a solid foundation for success.

Crafting Your Business Plan

A well-crafted business plan is the cornerstone of any successful food truck operation. It acts as a road plan for your company, detailing your objectives, tactics, and projected financials. Start by defining your mission and vision for your food truck business, and identify your target market, competitors, and unique value proposition. Outline your menu offerings, pricing strategy, and marketing plan, and establish clear objectives and milestones to measure your progress.

Personal Experience:
When I first decided to start a food truck business, I knew that creating a solid business plan was

essential for securing financing and guiding my decision-making process. I spent weeks researching the market, analyzing competitors, and refining my menu and concept. I outlined my goals, strategies, and financial projections in detail, taking into account factors such as startup costs, operating expenses, and revenue projections. By crafting a comprehensive business plan, I was able to clarify my vision for my food truck business and set myself up for success from the start.

Financial Planning and Budgeting

Financial planning and budgeting are critical aspects of managing a food truck business effectively. Start by estimating your startup costs, including expenses such as vehicle purchase or rental, equipment, permits and licenses, and initial inventory. Identify potential sources of funding, such as personal savings, loans, or investment capital, and create a detailed budget to track your expenses and cash flow. Monitor your financial performance regularly and adjust your budget as needed to ensure that you stay on track and achieve your financial goals.

Personal Experience:
Managing finances was one of the biggest challenges I faced when starting my food truck business. I had to carefully balance my budget to cover startup costs while also ensuring that I had enough capital to

sustain my business through the initial lean months. I tracked every expense meticulously, from equipment purchases to food inventory, and looked for ways to cut costs and increase efficiency wherever possible. By staying vigilant and proactive about my finances, I was able to weather the challenges of startup and position my food truck for long-term success.

Marketing and Promotion

Effective marketing and promotion are essential for attracting customers and generating buzz around your food truck business. Develop a marketing plan that outlines your target audience, messaging, and promotional strategies, including social media marketing, email campaigns, and community events. Build a strong online presence through social media platforms such as Instagram, Facebook, and Twitter, and engage with your audience regularly to build brand loyalty and awareness.

Personal Experience:
Marketing my food truck was a constant work in progress, requiring creativity, consistency, and perseverance. I leveraged social media platforms to showcase my menu offerings, share behind-the-scenes glimpses of my kitchen, and engage with customers in real-time. I collaborated with local businesses and organizations to host

pop-up events and food truck rallies, and participated in community festivals and farmers markets to reach new customers. By investing time and effort into marketing and promotion, I was able to build a loyal following and generate excitement around my food truck brand.

Adapting to Challenges and Opportunities

In the fast-paced world of food truck entrepreneurship, it's essential to remain agile and adaptable in the face of challenges and opportunities. Stay informed about industry trends and changes in consumer preferences, and be willing to pivot your business strategy as needed to stay ahead of the curve. Embrace feedback from customers and stakeholders, and use it as an opportunity to improve and innovate your offerings. By remaining flexible and open-minded, you can navigate the ups and downs of the food truck business and emerge stronger and more resilient in the long run.

Personal Experience:
Running a food truck business taught me the importance of flexibility and resilience in the face of adversity. I encountered numerous challenges along the way, from equipment breakdowns to inclement weather, but I learned to adapt quickly and find creative solutions to overcome obstacles. I listened

to feedback from customers and adjusted my menu and operations based on their preferences and suggestions. I also seized opportunities for growth and expansion, such as catering events and corporate partnerships, to diversify my revenue streams and expand my customer base. By embracing change and staying nimble in my approach, I was able to navigate the unpredictable landscape of the food truck industry and build a thriving business.

Conclusion

Business planning and financial management are critical components of building a successful food truck venture. By crafting a comprehensive business plan, managing your finances effectively, implementing strategic marketing and promotion, and remaining agile and adaptable in the face of challenges and opportunities, you can build a solid foundation for long-term success. Drawing from personal experiences and industry insights, you can create a roadmap for your food truck business that guides your decision-making and sets you up for growth and profitability in the competitive culinary landscape.

3.1 WRITING A BUSINESS PLAN

Crafting a comprehensive business plan is a foundational step in launching a successful food truck business. In this section, we'll break down the key components of a business plan and provide actionable insights to help you create a roadmap for your food truck venture.

1. Executive Summary

The executive summary is a concise overview of your food truck business plan, highlighting key elements such as your mission statement, target market, unique value proposition, and financial projections. It should provide a compelling introduction to your business and entice readers to delve deeper into the details of your plan.

What to Include:
- Mission statement: Clearly articulate the purpose and vision of your food truck business.
- Business concept: Describe your concept, cuisine, and target market.
- Unique value proposition: Highlight what sets your food truck apart from the competition.
- Financial summary: Provide a high-level overview of your startup costs, revenue projections, and expected profitability.

2. Company Description

The company description section provides more detailed information about your food truck business, including its history, legal structure, and ownership. It should provide context for readers to understand the background and context of your business.

What to Include:
- Business name and legal structure: Provide the legal name of your food truck business and specify its structure (e.g., sole proprietorship, partnership, LLC).
- Ownership and management: Detail the ownership structure and key members of your management team, including their roles and responsibilities.
- History and background: Share the backstory of your food truck business, including how the idea originated and any relevant milestones or achievements.

3. Market Analysis

The market analysis section examines the competitive landscape and target market for your food truck business. It should provide insights into industry trends, customer demographics, and competitor analysis to help you identify opportunities and challenges.

What to Include:
- Industry overview: Provide an overview of the food truck industry, including its growth trends, market size, and key drivers.
- Target market: Define your target market in terms of demographics, psychographics, and buying behavior.
- Competitive analysis: Identify and analyze your direct and indirect competitors, including their strengths, weaknesses, and market positioning.

4. Menu and Concept

The menu and concept section outlines your food offerings, culinary concept, and menu pricing strategy. It should showcase the uniqueness and appeal of your menu to attract customers and differentiate your food truck from competitors.

What to Include:
- Menu offerings: List and describe your menu items, including their ingredients, flavors, and pricing.
- Culinary concept: Explain the inspiration behind your culinary concept and how it reflects your brand's identity and values.
- Pricing strategy: Outline your pricing strategy, including how you determined menu prices based on factors such as ingredient costs, competition, and target market.

5. Marketing and Sales Strategy

The marketing and sales strategy section outlines how you plan to attract customers and generate revenue for your food truck business. It should include a mix of online and offline marketing tactics to reach your target audience effectively.

What to Include:
- Branding and positioning: Define your brand identity and positioning in the market, including your brand personality, values, and messaging.
- Promotion and advertising: Detail your promotional tactics, including social media marketing, email campaigns, and local advertising.
- Sales channels: Describe how you plan to sell your products, including on-site sales, catering services, and partnerships with local businesses.

6. Operations and Management

The operations and management section details the day-to-day operations and management structure of your food truck business. It should outline your operational processes, staffing requirements, and management team's responsibilities.

What to Include:
- Operational plan: Describe how your food truck will operate on a daily basis, including hours of operation, location selection, and logistics.
- Staffing plan: Outline your staffing requirements, including the number and roles of employees needed to run your food truck effectively.
- Management structure: Detail the organizational structure of your food truck business, including key management roles and responsibilities.

7. Financial Projections

The financial projections section presents your projected financial performance, including revenue, expenses, and profitability. It should provide a realistic assessment of your business's financial outlook and potential return on investment.

What to Include:
- Startup costs: Estimate the initial costs required to launch your food truck business, including vehicle purchase or rental, equipment, permits, and licenses.
- Revenue projections: Forecast your sales revenue based on factors such as menu pricing, customer volume, and market demand.
- Expense projections: Estimate your operating expenses, including food costs, labor, overhead, and marketing expenses.

- Profitability analysis: Calculate your projected profitability, including gross profit margins, net income, and return on investment.

Conclusion

Writing a business plan for your food truck business is a critical step in laying the groundwork for success. By addressing key elements such as your business concept, market analysis, menu and concept, marketing and sales strategy, operations and management, and financial projections, you can create a roadmap that guides your decision-making and sets you up for growth and profitability in the competitive food truck industry. Drawing from personal experiences and industry insights, you can create a compelling business plan that captures the essence of your food truck venture and demonstrates its potential for success.

3.2 BUDGETING AND FINANCIAL FORECASTING

Budgeting and financial forecasting are critical components of managing a successful food truck business. In this section, we'll explore the importance of budgeting, how to create a budget for your food truck, and the process of financial forecasting to help you plan for the future and make informed business decisions.

Why Budgeting Matters

Budgeting is the process of creating a financial plan that outlines your expected income and expenses over a specific period, typically a month, quarter, or year. It provides a roadmap for managing your finances and helps you allocate resources effectively to achieve your business goals. By creating a budget for your food truck, you can track your spending, identify areas of overspending or inefficiency, and make adjustments to improve your financial performance.

Creating a Budget

To create a budget for your food truck, start by listing all of your anticipated expenses, including both fixed and variable costs. Fixed costs are expenses that remain constant regardless of your sales volume, such as vehicle lease or loan payments, insurance, permits and licenses, and utilities. Variable costs, on the other hand, fluctuate with your sales volume and include expenses such as food inventory, fuel, labor, and marketing.

Once you've identified your expenses, estimate your monthly revenue based on factors such as menu prices, average sales volume, and operating hours. Deduct your expenses from your revenue to calculate your net profit or loss for the month. To make sure you stay on course and meet your financial objectives, review your budget frequently and make any necessary adjustments.

Financial Forecasting

Financial forecasting involves projecting your future financial performance based on past trends, current market conditions, and anticipated changes in your business environment. It helps you anticipate potential challenges and opportunities and plan accordingly to mitigate risks and capitalize on opportunities for growth. By forecasting your financial performance, you can make informed decisions about resource allocation, pricing strategies, and expansion plans to maximize your profitability and long-term success.

To create a financial forecast for your food truck, start by analyzing historical financial data, such as sales revenue, expenses, and profit margins. Identify trends and patterns in your data, such as seasonal fluctuations in sales or changes in customer preferences, and use this information to project your future performance. Consider external factors that may impact your business, such as economic conditions, industry trends, and competitive dynamics, and adjust your forecast accordingly.

Key Components of a Financial Forecast

A financial forecast typically includes the following key components:

1. Sales Forecast: Projected sales revenue based on factors such as menu prices, customer volume, and market demand.

2. Expense Forecast: Projected operating expenses, including food costs, labor, overhead, and marketing expenses.

3. Profit and Loss Forecast: Projected net profit or loss for the period, calculated by subtracting total expenses from total revenue.

4. Cash Flow Forecast: Projected cash inflows and outflows, including cash sales, expenses, and loan repayments, to ensure that you have sufficient liquidity to meet your financial obligations.

5. Break-Even Analysis: Calculation of the sales volume needed to cover your fixed and variable costs and break even, indicating the minimum level of sales required to achieve profitability.

Benefits of Financial Forecasting

Financial forecasting offers several benefits for your food truck business, including:

- Strategic Planning: Helps you identify opportunities for growth and expansion and allocate resources effectively to achieve your business goals.
- Risk Management: Allows you to anticipate potential challenges and risks and develop contingency plans to mitigate their impact on your business.
- Resource Allocation: Helps you make informed decisions about resource allocation, such as staffing levels, inventory management, and marketing spending, to optimize your profitability.
- Performance Monitoring: Provides a benchmark for evaluating your actual financial performance against your forecasted targets and identifying areas for improvement.

Conclusion

Budgeting and financial forecasting are essential tools for managing a successful food truck business. By creating a budget to track your income and expenses and forecasting your financial performance to plan for the future, you can make informed decisions that maximize your profitability and long-term success. Drawing from personal experiences and industry insights, you can develop a sound financial strategy that helps you achieve your business goals and navigate the challenges of the competitive food truck industry with confidence.

3.3 FUNDING YOUR FOOD TRUCK VENTURE

Securing funding is a crucial step in launching your food truck venture. In this section, we'll explore various sources of funding available to food truck entrepreneurs and provide actionable insights to help you finance your business effectively.

1. Personal Savings

One of the most popular methods for financing a food truck business is using personal savings. If you have savings set aside for this purpose, it can provide a reliable source of capital without the need to rely on external financing. Consider how much of your savings you're willing to invest in your business and weigh the risks and rewards carefully before making a decision.

2. Friends and Family

Another option for funding your food truck venture is to seek investment from friends and family members. This can be a more flexible and accessible source of capital compared to traditional lenders or investors. However, it's essential to approach this option with caution and ensure that you have a clear agreement in place to avoid potential conflicts or misunderstandings down the line.

3. Small Business Loans

Small business loans are a common financing option for food truck entrepreneurs. These loans are typically offered by banks, credit unions, or online lenders and can provide the capital you need to launch or expand your food truck business. Before applying for a loan, consider factors such as interest rates, repayment terms, and eligibility criteria to find the best option for your needs.

4. Crowdfunding

Crowdfunding platforms offer another avenue for food truck entrepreneurs to raise capital for their ventures. Websites such as Kickstarter, Indiegogo, and GoFundMe allow you to create a campaign to attract donations or investments from individuals who support your business idea. Crowdfunding can be an effective way to generate buzz around your food truck concept and raise funds from a wide audience.

5. Grants and Incentive Programs

Some government agencies, nonprofit organizations, and industry associations offer grants and incentive programs to support small businesses, including food truck ventures. These programs may provide funding, technical assistance, or other resources to help you launch or grow your business. Research available grant opportunities and eligibility requirements in your area to see if you qualify for financial assistance.

6. Equipment Financing

If you need to purchase or lease equipment for your food truck, equipment financing can help you spread out the cost over time. This type of financing allows you to borrow funds to purchase equipment and repay the loan over a set period, typically with fixed monthly payments. Consider factors such as interest rates, repayment terms, and equipment requirements when exploring equipment financing options.

7. Business Partnerships

Forming partnerships with other businesses or investors can provide additional capital and resources to support your food truck venture. Consider partnering with local restaurants, food suppliers, or event organizers to collaborate on menu offerings, marketing promotions, or event sponsorships. Be clear about the terms of the partnership and ensure that all parties are aligned in their goals and expectations.

8. Bootstrapping

Bootstrapping involves funding your food truck venture through revenue generated from sales rather than relying on external financing. While this approach requires a longer time horizon to reach profitability, it allows you to retain full ownership and control of your business. Consider strategies such as starting small, minimizing expenses, and reinvesting profits to bootstrap your food truck business from the ground up.

Conclusion

Funding your food truck venture requires careful planning, research, and consideration of various financing options available to you. By exploring sources such as personal savings, friends and family, small business loans, crowdfunding, grants and incentives, equipment financing, business partnerships, and bootstrapping, you can find the right combination of capital and resources to launch and grow your food truck business successfully. Drawing from personal experiences and industry insights, you can develop a sound financial strategy that aligns with your goals and sets you up for long-term success in the competitive food truck industry.

3.4 PRICING STRATEGY AND REVENUE MODELS

Developing a sound pricing strategy is essential for the success of your food truck business. In this section, we'll explore various pricing strategies and revenue models to help you set prices that maximize profitability while remaining competitive in the market.

1. Cost-Plus Pricing

Cost-plus pricing is a straightforward method of setting prices based on the cost of producing your menu items plus a markup to cover overhead and profit. Start by calculating the cost of ingredients, labor, and overhead for each menu item, then add a percentage markup to determine the final selling price. This approach ensures that your prices cover your costs and generate a profit margin on each sale.

2. Competitive Pricing

Competitive pricing involves setting prices based on what your competitors are charging for similar menu items. Research the prices of food trucks and restaurants in your area to understand the market rates and adjust your prices accordingly to remain competitive. While competitive pricing can help attract customers, be mindful of maintaining a balance between pricing and profitability to ensure your business's long-term viability.

3. Value-Based Pricing

Value-based pricing focuses on the perceived value of your menu items to customers rather than the cost of production or competitive rates. Determine the unique value proposition of your food truck, such as the quality of ingredients, portion sizes, or convenience, and set prices based on the value that customers place on these attributes. This approach allows you to capture the value you provide to customers and potentially command higher prices than your competitors.

4. Dynamic Pricing

Dynamic pricing involves adjusting prices in real-time based on factors such as demand, time of day, or special events. For example, you may offer discounted prices during off-peak hours to attract customers or increase prices during peak periods when demand is high. Dynamic pricing allows you to optimize revenue by aligning prices with customer demand and maximizing sales opportunities.

5. Bundle Pricing

Bundle pricing involves offering menu items as part of a bundle or combo deal at a discounted price compared to purchasing items individually. This strategy encourages customers to purchase multiple items and increases the average transaction value per customer. Consider bundling complementary menu items such as a sandwich, side dish, and drink or offering meal deals for groups to attract customers and boost sales.

6. Subscription or Membership Models

Subscription or membership models involve offering customers access to exclusive benefits or discounts in exchange for a recurring fee. For example, you may offer a loyalty program where customers pay a monthly or annual fee to receive discounts on menu items, access to special events, or rewards for frequent visits. This model can help foster customer loyalty and generate recurring revenue for your food truck business.

7. Event or Catering Services

In addition to selling individual menu items, consider offering event or catering services as an additional revenue stream for your food truck business. Catering events such as weddings, corporate functions, or private parties can provide opportunities to generate higher revenue per event and reach new customers. Develop customizable catering packages and pricing options to meet the needs of different clients and occasions.

Conclusion

Pricing strategy plays a critical role in the success of your food truck business, influencing sales volume, revenue, and profitability. By exploring different pricing strategies and revenue models such as cost-plus pricing, competitive pricing, value-based pricing, dynamic pricing, bundle pricing, subscription or membership models, and event or catering services, you can find the right approach to maximize profitability while remaining competitive in the market. Drawing from personal experiences and industry insights, you can develop a pricing strategy that aligns with your business goals and customer preferences, setting your food truck up for long-term success in the competitive culinary landscape.

CHAPTER 4:

LEGAL AND REGULATORY CONSIDERATIONS

Navigating the legal and regulatory landscape is essential for the success of your food truck business. In this chapter, we'll explore the key legal and regulatory considerations you need to be aware of, from permits and licenses to health and safety regulations, to ensure compliance and protect your business.

1. Permits and Licenses

Before hitting the road with your food truck, you'll need to obtain various permits and licenses to operate legally. These may include:

- Business License: A general business license is required to operate any business legally. Check with your local government or municipality to obtain the necessary permits.

- Food Service Permit: A food service permit is essential for handling and selling food safely. It ensures that your food truck complies with health and safety regulations and undergoes regular inspections.

- Parking Permit: Depending on your location, you may need a parking permit to operate your food truck in specific areas or at events. Research local parking regulations and obtain the necessary permits to avoid fines or penalties.

Personal Experience:
When I started my food truck business, obtaining permits and licenses was one of the first steps I took to ensure compliance with local regulations. I reached out to my city's business licensing department to understand the requirements and process for obtaining permits. It took some time and paperwork, but securing the necessary permits gave me peace of mind knowing that I was operating legally.

2. Health and Safety Regulations

Food safety is paramount in the food truck industry to protect the health and well-being of your customers. Familiarize yourself with health and safety regulations, including:

- Food Handling Guidelines: Follow proper food handling practices to prevent contamination and foodborne illnesses. This includes storing food at the correct temperatures, practicing good hygiene, and avoiding cross-contamination.

- Sanitation Requirements: Keep your food truck clean and sanitized to maintain a safe and hygienic environment. Regularly clean and disinfect surfaces, equipment, and utensils, and dispose of waste properly to prevent health hazards.

- Allergen Labeling: Clearly label menu items containing common allergens such as nuts, dairy, and gluten to inform customers with food allergies and prevent allergic reactions.

Personal Experience:
Maintaining high standards of cleanliness and food safety was a top priority for my food truck business. I implemented strict sanitation protocols and trained my staff on proper food handling practices to ensure compliance with health and safety regulations. Regular inspections and audits helped me identify areas for improvement and ensure that my food truck consistently met industry standards.

3. Tax Obligations

Understanding your tax obligations is crucial for managing your finances and staying compliant with tax laws. Some tax considerations for food truck businesses include:

- Sales Tax: Collect and remit sales tax on taxable sales of food and beverages. Keep accurate records of sales transactions and report sales tax to the appropriate tax authorities.

- Income Tax: Report business income and expenses on your tax return and pay income tax on any profits generated by your food truck business. Consult with a tax professional to ensure that you're taking advantage of any available deductions or credits.

- Employment Taxes: If you have employees, withhold and pay payroll taxes such as Social Security and Medicare taxes, federal and state income tax withholding, and unemployment taxes.

Personal Experience:
Managing taxes can be complex for small business owners, so I sought guidance from a tax advisor to ensure that I understood my tax obligations as a food truck operator. Keeping accurate financial records and staying organized helped me track income and expenses throughout the year, making tax time less stressful and ensuring compliance with tax laws.

4. Insurance Coverage

Protecting your food truck business with the right insurance coverage is essential to mitigate risks and liabilities. Consider the following types of insurance:

- General Liability Insurance: Provides coverage for bodily injury, property damage, and legal expenses resulting from accidents or injuries on your food truck premises.

- Commercial Auto Insurance: Covers damages to your food truck and liability for accidents while driving or parked.

- Product Liability Insurance: Protects against claims related to foodborne illnesses or injuries caused by your food products.

- Workers' compensation insurance: Offers benefits to staff members who suffer illnesses or injuries while working.

Personal Experience:
Investing in insurance coverage gave me peace of mind knowing that my food truck business was protected against unforeseen risks and liabilities. I worked with an insurance agent to assess my needs and customize a policy that provided comprehensive

coverage for my business operations, employees, and customers.

Conclusion

Understanding and complying with legal and regulatory requirements are essential for the success and longevity of your food truck business. By obtaining the necessary permits and licenses, adhering to health and safety regulations, fulfilling tax obligations, and securing insurance coverage, you can protect your business and reputation while focusing on delivering delicious food and excellent service to your customers. Drawing from personal experiences and industry insights, you can navigate the legal and regulatory landscape with confidence and ensure that your food truck business operates smoothly and compliantly in the competitive culinary market.

4.1 LICENSING AND PERMITS

Obtaining the necessary licenses and permits is a critical step in starting and operating a food truck business. In this section, we'll explore the various licenses and permits you'll need to ensure compliance with local regulations and operate your food truck legally.

1. Business License

To lawfully operate any kind of business, one must first obtain a business license. It grants you the authority to conduct business activities within a specific jurisdiction and ensures you comply with local regulations. To obtain a business license for your food truck, you'll need to apply through your city or county government. The application process may vary depending on your location, but typically involves filling out a form, paying a fee, and providing information about your business, such as its name, address, and legal structure.

2. Food Service Permit

A food service permit is essential for handling and selling food safely from your food truck. It ensures that your food truck complies with health and safety regulations and undergoes regular inspections to maintain food safety standards. To obtain a food service permit, you'll need to submit an application to your local health department or regulatory agency. The application process may require you to provide documentation such as a menu, food handling procedures, and proof of compliance with sanitation requirements. Once approved, you'll receive a permit that allows you to operate your food truck legally.

3. Parking Permit

Depending on your location, you may need a parking permit to operate your food truck in specific areas or at events. Parking regulations vary by city and may include restrictions on where food trucks can park, how long they can stay in one location, and whether they require special permits for events or festivals. Research local parking regulations and obtain the necessary permits to ensure that you can park your food truck legally without risking fines or penalties.

4. Health Department Inspections

Health department inspections are a crucial part of obtaining and maintaining a food service permit for your food truck. Health inspectors conduct routine inspections to ensure that your food truck meets sanitation and food safety standards and complies with health regulations. Inspections may cover various aspects of your food truck operation, including food storage and handling practices, cleanliness and sanitation of equipment and facilities, and employee hygiene. Prepare for inspections by implementing proper food safety protocols, maintaining a clean and organized food truck, and addressing any issues or violations promptly to ensure compliance and maintain your food service permit.

5. Special Permits and Endorsements

In addition to basic business and food service permits, you may need special permits or endorsements depending on the nature of your food truck business. For example, if you plan to serve alcohol from your food truck, you'll need to obtain a separate permit or endorsement for alcohol service. Similarly, if you plan to operate in multiple locations or participate in events outside your regular operating area, you may need additional permits or endorsements to comply with local regulations. Research the specific requirements for your business model and location to ensure that you obtain all necessary permits and endorsements to operate legally.

Personal Experience:

When I started my food truck business, navigating the permit and licensing process was a daunting task. I reached out to my local government and health department to understand the requirements and procedures for obtaining permits. By carefully following the application process and ensuring that my food truck met all health and safety standards, I was able to obtain the necessary permits and launch my business with confidence.

Conclusion

Licensing and permits are essential for operating a food truck business legally and ensuring compliance with local regulations. By obtaining the necessary licenses and permits, including a business license, food service permit, parking permit, and any special permits or endorsements required for your business model, you can Drive your food truck with assurance and tranquility of mind. Drawing from personal experiences and industry insights, you can navigate the permit and licensing process successfully and focus on delivering delicious food and excellent service to your customers while staying compliant with legal requirements.

4.2 HEALTH AND SAFETY REGULATIONS

Ensuring the health and safety of your customers is paramount when operating a food truck business. In this section, we'll delve into the essential health and safety regulations you need to adhere to, covering food handling practices, sanitation requirements, and employee hygiene protocols.

1. Food Handling Practices

Proper food handling practices are crucial for preventing contamination and foodborne illnesses. Follow these guidelines to maintain food safety standards:

- Storage: Store food at the correct temperatures to prevent bacterial growth. Refrigerate perishable items promptly and keep raw meat, poultry, and seafood separate from ready-to-eat foods to avoid cross-contamination.

- Preparation: Wash hands thoroughly with soap and water before handling food and between tasks to prevent the spread of bacteria. Use separate cutting boards and utensils for raw and cooked foods, and cook food to the appropriate temperature to kill harmful bacteria.

- Service: Serve food promptly after cooking to minimize the time it spends in the temperature danger zone (40°F to 140°F). Use clean serving utensils and avoid touching ready-to-eat food with bare hands to prevent contamination.

2. Sanitation Requirements

Maintaining a clean and sanitary food truck is essential for preventing foodborne illnesses and ensuring customer safety. Follow these sanitation requirements:

- Cleaning: Clean and sanitize all surfaces, equipment, and utensils regularly to remove dirt, grease, and bacteria. Use approved sanitizers and follow manufacturer instructions for proper cleaning and disinfection.

- Storage: Store food and supplies off the floor and away from potential contaminants. Use food-grade containers and packaging to prevent contamination and protect food from pests.

- Waste Disposal: Properly dispose of waste and garbage to prevent odors, attract pests, and maintain a clean environment. Use leak-proof trash bins with tight-fitting lids and empty them regularly to prevent overflow.

3. Employee Hygiene Protocols

Employee hygiene plays a crucial role in preventing the spread of foodborne illnesses. Implement these hygiene protocols to ensure the health and safety of your staff and customers:

- Handwashing: Require employees to wash their hands frequently with soap and water, especially after using the restroom, handling raw meat or poultry, and touching their face or hair. Provide handwashing stations with soap, water, and single-use towels for hand drying.

- Personal Protective Equipment (PPE): Provide employees with appropriate PPE such as gloves, hairnets, and aprons to minimize the risk of contamination. Ensure that PPE is worn correctly and replaced regularly to maintain effectiveness.

- Illness Policies: Implement policies that require employees to report any symptoms of illness and exclude them from work if they are sick. Train staff on the importance of staying home when ill and provide paid sick leave to encourage compliance with illness policies.

Personal Experience:

When I started my food truck business, implementing health and safety protocols was a top priority. I trained my staff on proper food handling practices, sanitation requirements, and employee hygiene protocols to ensure compliance with health regulations. Regular inspections and audits helped me identify areas for improvement and maintain high standards of cleanliness and safety in my food truck operation.

Conclusion

Adhering to health and safety regulations is essential for maintaining the trust and confidence of your customers and protecting the reputation of your food truck business. By following proper food handling practices, sanitation requirements, and employee hygiene protocols, you can prevent foodborne illnesses and ensure a safe and enjoyable dining experience for your customers. Drawing from personal experiences and industry insights, you can create a culture of food safety in your food truck operation and demonstrate your commitment to customer health and well-being.

4.3 INSURANCE FOR FOOD TRUCKS

Insurance is a vital aspect of protecting your food truck business from unexpected risks and liabilities. In this section, we'll explore the types of insurance coverage you need to consider, key factors to keep in mind when selecting insurance policies, and strategies for managing insurance costs effectively.

1. General Liability Insurance

General liability insurance provides coverage for bodily injury, property damage, and legal expenses resulting from accidents or injuries that occur on your food truck premises. This coverage protects you from potential lawsuits and liability claims filed by customers, vendors, or other third parties. Typically, general liability insurance covers the following:

- Slip and fall accidents: If a customer slips and falls on your food truck premises and sustains injuries, general liability insurance can cover their medical expenses and any legal costs associated with the incident.

- Property damage: If your food truck accidentally damages someone else's property, such as a vehicle or storefront, general liability insurance can cover the costs of repair or replacement.

- Product liability: If a customer becomes ill or injured due to consuming food from your food truck, general liability insurance can provide coverage for legal expenses and damages resulting from a product liability claim.

2. Commercial Auto Insurance

Commercial auto insurance is essential for protecting your food truck and liability for accidents while driving or parked. This coverage provides financial protection in the event of vehicle damage, bodily injury, or property damage resulting from accidents involving your food truck. Commercial auto insurance typically includes coverage for:

- Collision: Covers the cost of repairs or replacement if your food truck is damaged in a collision with another vehicle or object.

- Liability: Covers bodily injury and property damage liability for accidents caused by your food truck, such as collisions with other vehicles or pedestrians.

- Comprehensive: Covers non-collision-related damage to your food truck, such as theft, vandalism, or weather-related damage.

3. Product Liability Insurance

Product liability insurance is essential for food truck businesses to protect against claims related to foodborne illnesses or injuries caused by consuming food products. This coverage provides financial protection in the event of legal expenses and damages resulting from product liability claims. Product liability insurance typically includes coverage for:

- Foodborne illnesses: If a customer becomes ill after consuming food from your food truck and files a lawsuit alleging food poisoning, product liability insurance can cover legal expenses and damages resulting from the claim.

- Allergic reactions: If a customer experiences an allergic reaction after consuming food containing allergens not properly labeled, product liability insurance can provide coverage for legal expenses and damages resulting from the incident.

4. Workers' Compensation Insurance

Workers' compensation insurance is essential if you have employees working on your food truck. This coverage provides financial protection for employees who are injured or become ill while on the job. Workers' compensation insurance typically includes coverage for:

- Medical expenses: Covers medical treatment, rehabilitation, and prescription medications for employees injured on the job.

- Lost wages: Provides compensation for lost wages while employees are unable to work due to a work-related injury or illness.

- Disability benefits: Provides financial support for employees who suffer a temporary or permanent disability as a result of a work-related injury or illness.

5. Tips for Managing Insurance Costs

While insurance is necessary for protecting your food truck business, there are strategies you can use to manage insurance costs effectively:

- Shop around: Compare quotes from multiple insurance providers to find the best coverage at the most competitive rates.

- Bundle policies: Consider bundling multiple insurance policies, such as general liability, commercial auto, and workers' compensation, with the same provider to qualify for discounts.

- Risk management: Implement risk management practices to reduce the likelihood of accidents, injuries, and insurance claims. This may include employee training, implementing safety protocols, and maintaining proper documentation.

- Review coverage regularly: Periodically review your insurance coverage to ensure that it meets the evolving needs of your food truck business. Adjust coverage limits and deductibles as necessary to optimize coverage and manage costs effectively.

Conclusion

Insurance is a critical component of protecting your food truck business from unexpected risks and liabilities. By obtaining the necessary insurance coverage, including general liability, commercial auto, product liability, and workers' compensation insurance, you can safeguard your business and assets from potential threats and ensure financial stability in case of harm or mishaps. Drawing from personal experiences and industry insights, you can make informed decisions about insurance coverage and manage insurance costs effectively to protect your food truck business and promote its long-term success.

4.4 TAXATION AND BUSINESS STRUCTURE

Understanding taxation and selecting the right business structure are crucial steps in managing the financial aspects of your food truck business. In this section, we'll explore taxation requirements for food truck businesses, different business structures to consider, and factors to keep in mind when making these decisions.

1. Taxation Requirements

As a food truck business owner, you'll need to comply with various taxation requirements at the federal, state, and local levels. For food truck enterprises, the following are important tax considerations:

- Income Tax: Food truck businesses are typically taxed as pass-through entities, meaning that business income is reported on the owner's personal tax return. Keep detailed records of your business income and expenses to accurately report your taxable income and take advantage of available deductions and credits.

- Sales Tax: Most states require food truck businesses to collect and remit sales tax on taxable sales of food and beverages. Register for a sales tax permit with your state's department of revenue and familiarize yourself with sales tax rates and regulations in your area to ensure compliance.

- Employment Taxes: If you have employees working on your food truck, you'll need to withhold and pay employment taxes such as Social Security and Medicare taxes, federal and state income tax withholding, and unemployment taxes. Familiarize yourself with your tax obligations as an employer and ensure that you comply with payroll tax requirements.

- Quarterly Estimated Taxes: Depending on your business income and tax liability, you may be required to make quarterly estimated tax payments to the IRS and state tax authorities. Calculate your estimated tax liability each quarter and make timely payments to avoid penalties and interest charges.

2. Business Structure

Selecting the right business structure is essential for managing taxation, liability, and operational flexibility. Here are some common business structures to consider for your food truck business:

- Sole Proprietorship: A sole proprietorship is the simplest and most common form of business structure for small businesses, including food truck operations. As a sole proprietor, you have full control and ownership of your business, but you're personally liable for business debts and obligations.

- Partnership: If you're starting a food truck business with one or more partners, a partnership structure may be appropriate. Partnerships offer shared ownership and management responsibilities, but each partner is personally liable for the partnership's debts and liabilities.

- Limited Liability Company (LLC): An LLC combines the liability protection of a corporation with the flexibility and tax benefits of a partnership. LLC owners, known as members, are protected from personal liability for business debts and obligations, and profits and losses are reported on the members' individual tax returns.

- Corporation: Forming a corporation provides the highest level of liability protection for business owners. Shareholders own the corporation, and directors and officers manage its affairs. Corporations are subject to double taxation, meaning that profits are taxed at both the corporate and individual levels.

3. Factors to Consider

When selecting a business structure for your food truck business, consider the following factors:

- Liability Protection: Choose a business structure that provides adequate protection against personal liability for business debts and obligations. LLCs and corporations offer limited liability protection for business owners, while sole proprietorships and partnerships expose owners to unlimited personal liability.

- Tax Implications: Consider the tax implications of each business structure and how they will affect your business's overall tax liability. Consult with a tax advisor to understand the tax advantages and disadvantages of each structure and determine the best option for your specific circumstances.

- Operational Flexibility: Evaluate the operational flexibility offered by each business structure, including management structure, decision-making authority, and ease of ownership transfer. Choose a structure that aligns with your long-term business goals and allows for future growth and expansion.

Personal Experience:

When I started my food truck business, I opted for a sole proprietorship due to its simplicity and ease of setup. However, as my business grew and I hired employees, I transitioned to an LLC to protect my personal assets and take advantage of tax benefits. Consulting with a tax advisor helped me understand the implications of each business structure and make an informed decision that aligned with my business goals.

Conclusion

Navigating taxation and selecting the right business structure are essential steps in managing the financial aspects of your food truck business. By understanding taxation requirements, including income tax, sales tax, and employment taxes, and selecting a business structure that offers liability protection, tax advantages, and operational flexibility, you can set your food truck business up for success. Drawing from personal experiences and industry insights, you can make informed decisions about taxation and business structure that support your long-term business goals and ensure financial stability and compliance in the competitive culinary market.

CHAPTER 5:

SOURCING INGREDIENTS AND SUPPLIERS

In the world of food trucks, sourcing high-quality ingredients is essential for creating delicious and memorable dishes that keep customers coming back for more. In this chapter, we'll explore the importance of sourcing ingredients and suppliers, strategies for finding reliable suppliers, and tips for managing ingredient costs effectively.

1. Importance of Sourcing Ingredients

The quality of ingredients used in your food truck dishes directly impacts the taste, freshness, and overall appeal of your menu offerings. Here's why sourcing ingredients is crucial:

- Flavor and Quality: Fresh, high-quality ingredients result in superior flavor and texture, elevating the taste of your dishes and delighting customers with every bite.

- Consistency: Consistent sourcing of ingredients ensures that your menu items taste the same each time, building customer trust and loyalty to your brand.

- Differentiation: Unique or locally sourced ingredients can set your food truck apart from competitors and attract customers seeking fresh, artisanal offerings.

2. Finding Reliable Suppliers

Finding reliable suppliers is key to ensuring a steady supply of quality ingredients for your food truck business. Here's how to find and vet potential suppliers:

- Local Markets: Explore local farmers' markets, specialty food stores, and artisanal producers in your area to discover unique, fresh ingredients that align with your menu concept.

- Online Platforms: Utilize online platforms and directories to research and connect with potential suppliers. Look for suppliers with positive reviews, transparent pricing, and a track record of reliability.

- Networking: Attend industry events, food festivals, and networking events to connect with other food truck operators and suppliers. Networking can provide valuable insights and recommendations for reputable suppliers in your area.

- Samples and Trials: Request samples or conduct product trials before committing to a supplier. Evaluate the quality, freshness, and consistency of ingredients to ensure they meet your standards and expectations.

3. Managing Ingredient Costs

Managing ingredient costs is essential for maintaining profitability and sustainability in your food truck business. Here are some tips for controlling ingredient costs effectively:

- Menu Planning: Plan your menu carefully to optimize ingredient usage and minimize waste. Choose versatile ingredients that can be used across multiple menu items to reduce inventory and storage costs.

- Seasonal Sourcing: Take advantage of seasonal ingredients when planning your menu. Seasonal produce is often more abundant and affordable, allowing you to offer fresh, seasonal dishes while reducing costs.

- Bulk Purchasing: Purchase ingredients in bulk to take advantage of volume discounts and lower unit costs. Consider forming purchasing cooperatives with other food truck operators to negotiate better prices with suppliers.

- Negotiation: Negotiate pricing and terms with suppliers to secure the best possible deals. Build strong relationships with suppliers based on mutual trust and transparency to facilitate ongoing cost savings.

Personal Experience:

When I started my food truck business, sourcing ingredients was a top priority to ensure the quality and freshness of my menu offerings. I invested time in researching and vetting suppliers, visiting local markets, and sampling products to find the best ingredients for my dishes. By forging partnerships with reliable suppliers and implementing cost-saving strategies, I was able to maintain high standards of quality while keeping ingredient costs manageable.

Conclusion

Sourcing ingredients and suppliers is a critical aspect of running a successful food truck business. By prioritizing quality, reliability, and cost-effectiveness in your ingredient sourcing efforts, you can create delicious, memorable dishes that keep customers coming back for more. Drawing from personal experiences and industry insights, you can build a network of trusted suppliers, manage ingredient costs effectively, and differentiate your food truck business in the competitive culinary landscape.

5.1 BUILDING RELATIONSHIPS WITH SUPPLIERS

Establishing strong relationships with suppliers is essential for ensuring a steady supply of high-quality ingredients for your food truck business. In this section, we'll explore the importance of building relationships with suppliers, strategies for fostering mutual trust and collaboration, and the benefits of long-term supplier partnerships.

1. Importance of Supplier Relationships

Building relationships with suppliers goes beyond simply securing ingredient deliveries; it's about cultivating partnerships based on trust, communication, and mutual benefit. Here's why supplier relationships are crucial:

- Reliability: A strong relationship with suppliers ensures reliable and consistent deliveries of quality ingredients, reducing the risk of disruptions to your food truck operations.

- Flexibility: Suppliers who know and understand your business can accommodate special requests, provide customized solutions, and adapt to your changing needs more effectively.

- Cost Savings: Long-term relationships with suppliers often lead to cost savings through volume discounts, negotiated pricing, and preferential treatment, ultimately improving your bottom line.

2. Strategies for Building Relationships

Building strong relationships with suppliers requires proactive communication, transparency, and a genuine commitment to mutual success. Here are some strategies for fostering positive supplier relationships:

- Open Communication: Establish clear lines of communication with your suppliers and maintain regular contact to discuss orders, deliveries, and any issues or concerns that may arise. Be proactive in sharing feedback and updates to foster transparency and trust.

- Mutual Respect: Treat your suppliers with respect and professionalism, recognizing their expertise and value to your business. Show appreciation for their efforts, responsiveness, and commitment to meeting your needs.

- Consistency: Be consistent in your orders, payments, and business practices to demonstrate reliability and reliability to your suppliers. Consistency builds trust and confidence in your partnership and encourages suppliers to prioritize your business.

- Collaboration: Involve suppliers in your menu planning and product development processes, seeking their input and expertise to optimize ingredient selection, sourcing, and usage. Collaborative partnerships foster innovation and creativity while strengthening relationships.

3. Benefits of Long-Term Partnerships

Long-term partnerships with suppliers offer numerous benefits for your food truck business, including:

- Stability: Long-term relationships provide stability and predictability in your supply chain, reducing the risk of disruptions and ensuring continuity in ingredient availability.

- Quality Assurance: Suppliers who understand your business and preferences can consistently deliver high-quality ingredients that meet your standards and exceed customer expectations.

- Cost Efficiency: Long-term partnerships often result in cost savings through negotiated pricing, volume discounts, and streamlined processes, improving your profitability and competitiveness.

- Innovation: Collaborating with trusted suppliers can lead to innovative product offerings, menu enhancements, and operational efficiencies that drive growth and differentiation in your food truck business.

Personal Experience:

When I started my food truck business, I recognized the importance of building strong relationships with suppliers to ensure the success and sustainability of my operation. I invested time and effort in cultivating partnerships based on trust, communication, and mutual respect, and I saw firsthand the benefits of long-term supplier relationships. By working closely with suppliers, I was able to secure reliable ingredient deliveries, access cost-effective pricing, and introduce innovative menu items that delighted customers and drove business growth.

Conclusion

Building relationships with suppliers is a fundamental aspect of running a successful food truck business. By prioritizing open communication, mutual respect, and collaboration, you can establish strong partnerships that drive operational excellence, ensure ingredient quality, and support long-term growth and profitability. Drawing from personal experiences and industry insights, you can cultivate supplier relationships that serve as the foundation for your food truck business's success and resilience in the dynamic culinary landscape.

5.2 ENSURING QUALITY AND CONSISTENCY

Maintaining consistent quality in your food offerings is paramount to the success of your food truck business. In this section, we'll delve into strategies for ensuring quality and consistency in your ingredients, recipes, and customer experience, highlighting the importance of attention to detail, training, and quality control measures.

1. Quality Ingredients

Quality ingredients are the foundation of delicious and memorable food. Here's how to ensure the quality of your ingredients:

- Sourcing: Partner with reputable suppliers who provide fresh, high-quality ingredients that meet your standards. Conduct regular quality checks on incoming ingredients to ensure freshness, flavor, and consistency.

- Storage: Properly store ingredients at the correct temperature and humidity levels to maintain freshness and prevent spoilage. Use first-in, first-out (FIFO) inventory management to rotate stock and minimize waste.

- Handling: Train your staff on proper handling techniques to prevent contamination and preserve ingredient integrity. Emphasize the importance of cleanliness, hygiene, and sanitation in all food preparation processes.

2. Consistent Recipes

Consistency in recipes ensures that your customers receive the same great taste every time they visit your food truck. Here's how to maintain consistency in your recipes:

- Standardization: Develop standardized recipes with precise measurements and instructions for each menu item. Train your kitchen staff on recipe execution and portion control to ensure uniformity across all dishes.

- Quality Control: Implement quality control measures, such as taste tests and visual inspections, to monitor the consistency of your dishes. Solicit feedback from customers and staff to identify any deviations from the desired flavor profile or presentation.

- Ingredient Substitutions: Document any necessary ingredient substitutions or modifications to recipes and communicate them clearly to your kitchen staff. Ensure that substitutions maintain the integrity of the dish while accommodating dietary restrictions or ingredient availability.

3. Customer Experience

Consistency in the customer experience is key to building trust, loyalty, and repeat business. Here's how to deliver a consistent customer experience:

- Service Standards: Establish service standards and protocols for greeting customers, taking orders, and delivering food. Train your front-of-house staff on customer service etiquette, communication skills, and problem-solving techniques to ensure a positive dining experience.

- Speed and Efficiency: Streamline your operations to minimize wait times and maximize efficiency during peak hours. Optimize workflow, staffing levels, and equipment placement to facilitate quick and seamless service without compromising quality.

- Feedback Mechanisms: Encourage customer feedback through comment cards, online reviews, and social media channels. Use feedback to identify areas for improvement and address any issues or concerns promptly and professionally.

Personal Experience:

In my food truck business, ensuring quality and consistency was a top priority from day one. I invested time and resources in sourcing the freshest ingredients, developing standardized recipes, and training my staff to execute them with precision and consistency. By maintaining rigorous quality control measures and prioritizing the customer experience, I was able to build a loyal customer base and differentiate my food truck in a competitive market.

Conclusion

Ensuring quality and consistency in your food truck business requires careful attention to detail, rigorous quality control measures, and a commitment to delivering exceptional customer experiences. By sourcing high-quality ingredients, standardizing recipes, and training your staff effectively, you can maintain consistency in your food offerings and build trust and loyalty with your customers. Drawing from personal experiences and industry insights, you can create a dining experience that delights customers and keeps them coming back to your food truck time and time again.

5.3 SUSTAINABLE SOURCING PRACTICES

In today's increasingly environmentally conscious world, implementing sustainable sourcing practices is not only beneficial for the planet but also for your food truck business. In this section, we'll explore the importance of sustainable sourcing, practical strategies for incorporating sustainability into your ingredient sourcing, and the financial benefits of adopting eco-friendly practices.

1. Importance of Sustainable Sourcing

Sustainable sourcing involves choosing ingredients and suppliers that prioritize environmental responsibility, social equity, and ethical production practices. Here's why sustainable sourcing is important for your food truck business:

- Environmental Impact: By sourcing ingredients from sustainable sources, you can reduce your carbon footprint, minimize resource depletion, and protect natural ecosystems and biodiversity.

- Consumer Demand: Today's consumers are increasingly mindful of the environmental and social impact of their purchasing decisions. By offering sustainably sourced menu items, you can appeal to environmentally conscious customers and differentiate your food truck in a competitive market.

- Long-Term Viability: Adopting sustainable sourcing practices not only benefits the planet but also contributes to the long-term viability and resilience of your business. By reducing waste, conserving resources, and supporting sustainable agriculture, you can future-proof your food truck against environmental and economic challenges.

2. Practical Strategies for Sustainable Sourcing

Incorporating sustainability into your ingredient sourcing requires a multifaceted approach that considers environmental, social, and economic factors. Here are some practical strategies for implementing sustainable sourcing practices in your food truck business:

- Local and Seasonal Ingredients: Source ingredients locally and seasonally whenever possible to reduce transportation emissions and support local farmers and producers. Visit farmers' markets, join community-supported agriculture (CSA) programs, and build relationships with local suppliers to access fresh, seasonal ingredients.

- Organic and Fair Trade: Choose organic and fair trade ingredients to support sustainable farming practices, promote soil health, and ensure fair wages and working conditions for agricultural workers. Look for certifications such as USDA Organic and Fair Trade Certified to verify the authenticity of your ingredients.

- Reducing Food Waste: Implement measures to reduce food waste in your food truck operations, such as portion control, menu planning, and composting organic waste. Donate surplus food to local food banks or shelters to minimize landfill waste and support community food security initiatives.

- Packaging and Waste Reduction: Minimize single-use plastics and packaging waste by using eco-friendly alternatives such as compostable or biodegradable materials. Offer incentives for customers who bring their own reusable containers or utensils to reduce waste generated by takeout orders.

3. Financial Benefits of Sustainable Sourcing

While implementing sustainable sourcing practices may require upfront investment and operational changes, the long-term financial benefits far outweigh the costs. Here are some financial advantages of adopting sustainable sourcing practices:

- Cost Savings: Sustainable sourcing can lead to cost savings through reduced energy consumption, lower waste disposal costs, and optimized supply chain efficiencies. For example, sourcing locally and seasonally can reduce transportation costs and eliminate the need for expensive packaging and preservatives.

- Brand Reputation: A commitment to sustainability can enhance your brand reputation and attract environmentally conscious customers willing to pay a premium for ethically sourced, eco-friendly products. Building a loyal customer base through sustainability can drive sales and revenue growth over time.

- Regulatory Compliance: Embracing sustainable sourcing practices can help you stay ahead of evolving regulatory requirements and consumer expectations related to environmental and social responsibility. By proactively addressing sustainability issues, you can mitigate compliance risks and avoid potential fines or penalties.

Personal Experience:

In my food truck business, I made a conscious effort to prioritize sustainability in ingredient sourcing from the outset. By sourcing locally grown produce, organic meats, and fair trade coffee, I not only reduced my environmental footprint but also attracted environmentally conscious customers who appreciated my commitment to sustainability. Over time, sustainability became a core value of my brand, driving customer loyalty and contributing to the financial success of my business.

Conclusion

Sustainable sourcing practices are essential for ensuring the long-term success and sustainability of your food truck business. By choosing ingredients and suppliers that prioritize environmental responsibility, social equity, and ethical production practices, you can reduce your environmental footprint, appeal to environmentally conscious customers, and drive financial growth and profitability. Drawing from personal experiences and industry insights, you can implement practical strategies for sustainable sourcing that benefit both your business and the planet, positioning your food truck as a leader in sustainability in the culinary landscape.

5.4 MANAGING INVENTORY

Effective inventory management is crucial for the success of your food truck business. Properly managing inventory ensures that you have the right ingredients on hand to meet customer demand while minimizing waste and controlling costs. In this section, we'll explore practical strategies for managing inventory efficiently, reducing food waste, and optimizing your ingredient procurement processes.

1. Importance of Inventory Management

Inventory management plays a critical role in the day-to-day operations and financial health of your food truck business. Here's why it's important:

- Cost Control: Proper inventory management helps you control costs by minimizing excess inventory, reducing waste, and avoiding stockouts or overordering.

- Customer Satisfaction: Having the right ingredients available when customers order ensures a positive dining experience and helps build customer loyalty.

- Operational Efficiency: Efficient inventory management streamlines your operations, reduces labor costs associated with inventory handling, and improves overall productivity.

2. Strategies for Effective Inventory Management

Implementing effective inventory management practices requires careful planning, organization, and attention to detail. Here are some strategies to help you manage your food truck inventory efficiently:

- Regular Inventory Audits: Conduct regular inventory audits to track stock levels, identify slow-moving or expired items, and prevent overstocking. Use inventory management software or spreadsheets to keep accurate records of inventory levels and transactions.

- Forecasting and Planning: Use sales data and historical trends to forecast demand for ingredients and plan your inventory purchases accordingly. Adjust your inventory levels based on seasonality, special events, and anticipated changes in customer demand.

- Just-in-Time Ordering: Adopt a just-in-time (JIT) inventory management approach to minimize storage costs and reduce the risk of food spoilage. Order ingredients from suppliers only when needed to fulfill customer orders, rather than keeping large quantities of inventory on hand.

- Supplier Relationships: Build strong relationships with your suppliers to ensure reliable and timely deliveries of ingredients. Communicate your inventory needs and requirements to suppliers to minimize lead times and avoid stockouts.

3. Reducing Food Waste

Food waste is a significant challenge for food truck businesses, but effective inventory management can help minimize waste and maximize profitability. Here are some tips for reducing food waste in your food truck operations:

- Portion Control: Implement portion control measures to reduce over-portioning and minimize leftovers. Train your staff to portion ingredients accurately and use standardized recipes to maintain consistency.

- Menu Optimization: Analyze your menu regularly to identify low-performing items and adjust your offerings accordingly. Focus on selling high-margin menu items and avoid carrying excess inventory of slow-moving ingredients.

- Donations and Recycling: Donate surplus food to local food banks or charities to reduce waste and support community organizations. Compost organic waste to divert it from landfills and contribute to environmental sustainability.

4. Technology Solutions

Invest in inventory management software or point-of-sale (POS) systems with inventory tracking capabilities to streamline your inventory management processes. These tools can help you track inventory levels in real time, automate reordering, and generate reports to analyze inventory trends and performance.

Personal Experience:

In my food truck business, managing inventory was a constant challenge, especially in a fast-paced and dynamic environment. I found that implementing regular inventory audits and adopting a just-in-time ordering approach helped me control costs and reduce waste. By closely monitoring inventory levels and forecasting demand, I was able to optimize my ingredient procurement processes and ensure that I always had the right ingredients on hand to meet customer demand.

Conclusion

Effective inventory management is essential for the success and profitability of your food truck business. By implementing strategies to track inventory levels accurately, forecast demand, and minimize waste, you can control costs, improve operational efficiency, and enhance customer satisfaction. Drawing from personal experiences and industry best practices, you can develop a robust inventory management system that supports the long-term success and sustainability of your food truck business in the competitive culinary landscape.

CHAPTER 6:

MARKETING AND BRANDING STRATEGIES

Marketing and branding are essential components of building a successful food truck business. In this chapter, we'll explore effective strategies for promoting your food truck, building brand awareness, and attracting and retaining customers. Drawing from personal experiences and industry insights, we'll delve into practical tips and tactics to help you market your food truck effectively and stand out in a competitive market.

1. Importance of Marketing and Branding

Marketing and branding play a crucial role in shaping the perception of your food truck business and attracting customers. Here's why it's important to invest in marketing and branding:

- Brand Identity: Establishing a strong brand identity helps differentiate your food truck from competitors and creates a memorable impression in the minds of consumers.

- Customer Engagement: Effective marketing strategies engage customers and build relationships, fostering loyalty and repeat business.

- Business Growth: Well-executed marketing campaigns can drive awareness, generate leads, and ultimately contribute to the growth and success of your food truck business.

2. Crafting Your Brand Identity

Developing a strong brand identity is the foundation of your marketing efforts. Here's how to craft a compelling brand identity for your food truck:

- Define Your Unique Selling Proposition (USP): Identify what sets your food truck apart from competitors and articulate it clearly in your branding. Whether it's your unique menu offerings, culinary style, or commitment to sustainability, your USP should resonate with your target audience.

- Create a Memorable Logo and Visual Identity: Design a logo and visual elements that reflect your brand personality and appeal to your target demographic. Use consistent branding across all touchpoints, including signage, menus, social media, and promotional materials.

- Tell Your Story: Share the story behind your food truck, including your inspiration, values, and journey as a business owner. Authentic storytelling humanizes your brand and creates emotional connections with customers.

3. Marketing Strategies

Once you've established your brand identity, it's time to promote your food truck and attract customers. The following are some successful marketing techniques to think about:

- Social Media Marketing: Leverage platforms like Instagram, Facebook, and Twitter to showcase your menu offerings, share behind-the-scenes glimpses, and engage with your audience. Use high-quality visuals, hashtags, and user-generated content to enhance your social media presence.

- Local Partnerships and Events: Collaborate with local businesses, event organizers, and community organizations to participate in food festivals, pop-up markets, and other events. Networking with other vendors and sponsors can help increase your visibility and attract new customers.

- Email Marketing: Build an email list of loyal customers and subscribers and send regular updates, promotions, and exclusive offers. Personalize your emails based on customer preferences and behavior to maximize engagement and conversions.

4. Customer Experience and Retention

Delivering exceptional customer experiences is essential for retaining customers and building brand loyalty. Here are some tips to improve the clientele's experience:

- Consistent Quality and Service: Maintain high standards of food quality, presentation, and service to exceed customer expectations. Recurring business is encouraged and trust is built via consistency.

- Customer Feedback: Encourage feedback from customers through surveys, comment cards, and online reviews. Use feedback to identify areas for improvement and address any issues or concerns promptly.

- Loyalty Programs: Implement a loyalty program to reward repeat customers and incentivize future visits. Offer discounts, freebies, or exclusive perks to loyal customers to thank them for their support and encourage continued patronage.

Personal Experience:

In my food truck business, marketing and branding played a crucial role in driving awareness and attracting customers. I invested time and resources in developing a strong brand identity, including designing a memorable logo and establishing a cohesive visual identity across all marketing channels. By leveraging social media platforms, participating in local events, and prioritizing customer satisfaction, I was able to build a loyal customer base and differentiate my food truck in a competitive market.

Conclusion

Marketing and branding are essential components of building a successful food truck business. By crafting a compelling brand identity, implementing effective marketing strategies, and delivering exceptional customer experiences, you can attract and retain customers, drive business growth, and establish your food truck as a beloved culinary destination in your community. Drawing from personal experiences and industry best practices, you can develop a comprehensive marketing and branding strategy that resonates with your target audience and sets your food truck apart in a crowded marketplace.

6.1 CREATING A STRONG BRAND IDENTITY

Crafting a strong brand identity is essential for establishing a memorable and recognizable presence for your food truck business. In this section, we'll explore the key components of building a robust brand identity, including defining your unique selling proposition (USP), creating visual elements, and communicating your brand story effectively.

1. Define Your Unique Selling Proposition (USP)

Your unique selling proposition (USP) is what sets your food truck apart from competitors and resonates with your target audience. To define your USP:

- Identify Your Strengths: Analyze your menu offerings, culinary style, and business practices to identify what makes your food truck unique. Consider factors such as your specialty dishes, cooking techniques, sourcing practices, or commitment to sustainability.

- Understand Your Target Audience: Research your target demographic to understand their preferences, needs, and pain points. Tailor your USP to address specific customer desires and differentiate your food truck in the market.

- Articulate Your Value Proposition: Clearly articulate the value that your food truck provides to customers. Whether it's exceptional taste, innovative flavors, convenience, or a unique dining experience, your USP should communicate why customers should choose your food truck over competitors.

2. Create Visual Elements

Visual elements play a crucial role in communicating your brand identity and creating a memorable impression. To create effective visual elements:

- Design a Logo: Develop a logo that reflects your brand personality and resonates with your target audience. Your logo should be simple, versatile, and easily recognizable, whether displayed on signage, menus, or promotional materials.

- Choose Brand Colors and Fonts: Select a cohesive color palette and font style that aligns with your brand identity and enhances brand recognition. Consistent use of colors and fonts across all marketing materials reinforces brand cohesion and strengthens brand recall.

- Create Brand Collateral: Design branded collateral such as business cards, menus, and packaging that showcase your visual identity and reinforce your brand message. Ensure that all branding elements are consistent in style, tone, and quality.

3. Communicate Your Brand Story

Your brand story is the narrative that communicates your values, mission, and passion for food to your audience. To effectively communicate your brand story:

- Be Authentic: Share your authentic story and the journey behind your food truck, including your inspiration, background, and values. Authentic storytelling creates emotional connections with customers and fosters trust and loyalty.

- Highlight Your Unique Qualities: Emphasize what makes your food truck special, whether it's your family recipes, culinary heritage, or commitment to using locally sourced ingredients. Highlighting your unique qualities helps differentiate your brand and build a loyal customer base.

- Engage with Your Audience: Use storytelling techniques to engage with your audience across various marketing channels, including social media, website content, and promotional materials. Share behind-the-scenes glimpses, chef's tips, and customer testimonials to humanize your brand and connect with customers on a personal level.

Personal Experience:

In my food truck business, creating a strong brand identity was essential for standing out in a competitive market. I focused on defining a clear USP that highlighted our unique menu offerings and commitment to using fresh, locally sourced ingredients. We invested in professional logo design and branding materials that reflected our brand personality and values, and we consistently communicated our brand story through social media posts, blog content, and interactions with customers.

Conclusion

Creating a strong brand identity is key to building a successful food truck business. By defining your unique selling proposition, creating compelling visual elements, and communicating your brand story effectively, you can differentiate your food truck in the market, attract loyal customers, and drive business growth. Drawing from personal experiences and industry best practices, you can develop a cohesive brand identity that resonates with your target audience and sets your food truck apart as a beloved culinary destination in your community.

6.2 BUILDING AN ONLINE PRESENCE

In the current digital era, building a strong web presence is essential to your food truck business's success. An effective online presence not only increases your visibility and reach but also allows you to engage with your audience, build brand awareness, and drive customer traffic to your truck. In this section, we'll explore practical strategies for building an online presence that attracts customers and enhances your food truck's reputation.

1. Create a Professional Website

A professional website serves as the online hub for your food truck business and provides customers with essential information about your menu, location, hours of operation, and contact details. Here's how to create a compelling website for your food truck:

- Simple and User-Friendly Design: Design a clean and intuitive website layout that is easy to navigate on both desktop and mobile devices. Include high-quality images of your food offerings, truck exterior, and staff to showcase your brand personality.

- Menu Display: Clearly display your menu with mouthwatering photos, descriptions, and pricing. Organize your menu into categories for easy browsing and include any dietary information or special instructions for ordering.

- Location and Hours: Provide accurate information about your food truck's location, schedule, and upcoming events or promotions. Include a map with your current location and directions for customers to find you easily.

- Contact Information: Make it easy for customers to get in touch with you by including a contact form, email address, phone number, and links to your social media profiles.

2. Leverage Social Media Platforms

Social media platforms are powerful tools for connecting with your audience, sharing engaging content, and promoting your food truck business. Here's how to use social media to your advantage:

- Choose the Right Platforms: Identify the social media platforms where your target audience is most active, whether it's Instagram, Facebook, Twitter, or TikTok. Focus your efforts on the platforms that align with your brand and offer the best opportunities for engagement.

- Share Compelling Content: Create and share compelling content that showcases your food, behind-the-scenes moments, customer testimonials, and special promotions. Use high-quality photos and videos to capture attention and encourage interaction.

- Engage with Your Audience: Actively engage with your followers by responding to comments, messages, and reviews in a timely and professional manner. Encourage user-generated content by reposting customer photos and reviews and tagging them in your posts.

- Utilize Hashtags: Use relevant hashtags to increase the visibility of your posts and attract new followers. Research popular hashtags in the food and local community to reach a broader audience and increase engagement.

3. Online Ordering and Delivery

Offering online ordering and delivery services can enhance convenience for your customers and expand your reach beyond your physical location. Here's how to implement online ordering and delivery for your food truck:

- Choose a Platform: Select a reliable online ordering platform or mobile app that integrates seamlessly with your website and POS system. Choose a platform that offers customizable menus, order tracking, and delivery management features.

-Streamline Operations: Streamline your order fulfillment process to ensure smooth operations and timely delivery. Train your staff on order processing, packaging, and delivery protocols to maintain quality and consistency.

- Promote Online Ordering: Promote your online ordering and delivery services through your website, social media channels, and email newsletters. Offer incentives such as discounts or freebies for customers who place orders online to encourage adoption and repeat business.

Personal Experience:

In my food truck business, building an online presence was instrumental in reaching new customers and growing our customer base. We invested in a professional website that showcased our menu, location, and contact information, making it easy for customers to find and order from us. We also leveraged social media platforms like Instagram and Facebook to share mouthwatering photos of our dishes, engage with our audience, and promote special events and promotions. By offering online ordering and delivery services, we were able to expand our reach and cater to customers who preferred the convenience of ordering from their mobile devices.

Conclusion

Building an online presence is essential for the success of your food truck business in today's digital landscape. By creating a professional website, leveraging social media platforms, and offering online ordering and delivery services, you can increase your visibility, engage with your audience, and drive customer traffic to your truck. Drawing from personal experiences and industry best practices, you can develop a comprehensive online presence strategy that enhances your food truck's reputation and drives business growth in the competitive culinary market.

6.3 SOCIAL MEDIA MARKETING TACTICS

Social media marketing is a powerful tool for promoting your food truck business, engaging with your audience, and driving customer traffic to your truck. In this section, we'll explore effective social media marketing tactics to help you maximize your online presence and attract customers.

1. Define Your Social Media Goals

Before diving into social media marketing, it's essential to define clear goals and objectives for your efforts. Here are some common social media goals for food truck businesses:

- Increase brand awareness
- Drive traffic to your truck
- Boost engagement with your audience
- Generate leads and sales

By defining your goals upfront, you can tailor your social media strategy to achieve measurable outcomes and track your progress over time.

2. Choose the Right Platforms

Not all social media platforms are created equal, and it's essential to choose the platforms that best align with your target audience and business objectives. Here's a brief overview of popular social media platforms for food truck businesses:

- Instagram: Ideal for visual content such as mouthwatering food photos and behind-the-scenes glimpses of your truck. Use Instagram's features like Stories, Reels, and IGTV to engage with your audience creatively.

- Facebook: A versatile platform for sharing updates, events, and promotions with your followers. Create a Facebook Business Page to showcase your menu, location, and contact information and connect with your audience through posts, events, and live videos.

- Twitter: Great for real-time updates, customer interactions, and engaging in conversations with your audience. Use Twitter to share quick bites of information, respond to customer inquiries, and participate in trending topics and hashtags.

- TikTok: A rapidly growing platform known for its short-form videos and viral content. Create entertaining and engaging TikTok videos showcasing your food, staff, and truck to reach a younger demographic and tap into viral trends.

Choose the platforms that resonate most with your target audience and focus your efforts on creating engaging content that drives results.

3. Content Strategy

A solid content plan is the cornerstone of a profitable social media marketing campaign. Here's how to develop an effective content strategy for your food truck business:

- Create Compelling Visuals: High-quality, mouthwatering photos and videos are essential for grabbing attention and enticing customers to visit your truck. Invest in professional photography or learn basic photography techniques to capture your dishes in the best light.

- Showcase Your Menu: Use social media to showcase your menu offerings, daily specials, and seasonal promotions. Experiment with different formats such as carousel posts, slideshows, and videos to highlight your signature dishes and tempt your audience's taste buds.

- Share Behind-the-Scenes Content: Give your audience a glimpse behind the scenes of your food truck operation, including food preparation, staff interactions, and events. Real, behind-the-scenes footage gives your brand a human face and helps you gain your audience's trust.

- Engage with Your Audience: Actively engage with your audience by responding to comments, messages, and reviews in a timely and authentic manner. Encourage user-generated content by reposting customer photos and reviews and tagging them in your posts.

4. Promotional Tactics

Social media offers numerous opportunities for promoting your food truck and driving customer traffic. Here are some promotional tactics to consider:

- Run Contests and Giveaways: Host contests or giveaways on social media to encourage engagement and reward your followers. Offer prizes such as free meals, merchandise, or exclusive discounts for participating.

- Collaborate with Influencers: Partner with local influencers or food bloggers to showcase your food truck and reach a wider audience. Offer complimentary meals or exclusive experiences in exchange for social media mentions or reviews.

- Promote Special Events: Use social media to promote special events, pop-up locations, and promotions to your audience. Create event pages, share event details, and encourage followers to RSVP and spread the word.

- Use Paid Advertising: Consider using paid advertising on social media platforms to boost your reach and target specific demographics or geographic locations. Experiment with different ad formats such as sponsored posts, carousel ads, or video ads to see what resonates best with your audience.

5. Measure and Analyze Performance

Finally, it's essential to track and analyze the performance of your social media marketing efforts to understand what's working and what's not. Use social media analytics tools provided by each platform to track key metrics such as engagement, reach, impressions, and conversions. Use these insights to refine your strategy, optimize your content, and achieve your social media goals effectively.

Conclusion

Social media marketing offers food truck businesses a powerful platform for promoting their brand, engaging with their audience, and driving customer traffic to their trucks. By defining clear goals, choosing the right platforms, developing a compelling content strategy, and leveraging promotional tactics effectively, you can maximize your online presence and attract customers to your truck. Drawing from personal experiences and industry best practices, you can develop a comprehensive social media marketing strategy that enhances your food truck's reputation and drives business growth in the competitive culinary market.

6.4 EVENT MARKETING AND COLLABORATIONS

Event marketing and collaborations are effective strategies for food truck businesses to increase visibility, attract new customers, and generate buzz around their brand. In this section, we'll explore how to leverage event marketing and collaborations to maximize exposure and drive customer traffic to your food truck.

1. Identify Relevant Events

The first step in event marketing is to identify relevant events and opportunities where your food truck can participate. Consider the following types of events:

- Food Festivals: Participating in food festivals allows you to showcase your menu alongside other food vendors and attract a diverse audience of food enthusiasts.

- Community Events: Local community events such as fairs, markets, and fundraisers provide opportunities to connect with residents and support local causes while promoting your business.

- Corporate Events: Partnering with businesses or organizations to cater corporate events, office lunches, or private parties can be lucrative opportunities to showcase your catering services and reach a captive audience.

- Cultural Festivals: Cultural festivals celebrating specific cuisines or traditions offer opportunities to introduce your food to new audiences and align with the theme of the event.

2. Plan Your Participation

Once you've identified relevant events, it's essential to plan your participation effectively to maximize your impact and ensure a successful outcome. Here's what to consider:

- Event Logistics: Coordinate logistics such as event dates, location, setup requirements, and permits well in advance to ensure a smooth and seamless experience on the day of the event.

- Menu Selection: Tailor your menu to suit the event theme and audience preferences. Consider offering special menu items or promotions exclusive to the event to entice attendees to visit your food truck.

- Promotional Materials: Prepare promotional materials such as banners, signage, flyers, and branded merchandise to attract attention and reinforce your brand presence at the event.

- Staffing and Training: Ensure you have adequate staffing to handle the increased demand during the event. Train your staff on customer service, food handling, and upselling techniques to deliver an exceptional experience to event attendees.

3. Collaborate with Other Businesses

Collaborating with other businesses or organizations can amplify your marketing efforts and expand your reach to new audiences. Here are some collaboration ideas to consider:

- Cross-Promotions: Partner with complementary businesses such as local breweries, coffee shops, or dessert vendors to offer special promotions or discounts to each other's customers. Cross-promotions encourage mutual support and introduce your business to new audiences.

- Co-Branded Events: Organize co-branded events or pop-up collaborations with other food trucks, restaurants, or food-related businesses to create unique dining experiences and attract a broader customer base.

- Community Partnerships: Forge partnerships with local organizations, schools, or nonprofits to sponsor events, fundraisers, or community initiatives. Sponsorship opportunities provide visibility for your brand while supporting worthy causes and strengthening community ties.

4. Amplify Your Presence

To maximize the impact of your event marketing efforts, it's essential to amplify your presence before, during, and after the event. Here's how:

- Pre-Event Promotion: Use social media, email newsletters, and your website to promote your participation in upcoming events and generate excitement among your followers. Share sneak peeks of your menu, event details, and exclusive offers to encourage attendance.

- Live Coverage: During the event, leverage social media platforms to provide live coverage, behind-the-scenes glimpses, and real-time updates to engage with your audience and attract visitors to your food truck.

- Post-Event Follow-Up: After the event, follow up with attendees through social media posts, email newsletters, or thank-you notes to express gratitude for their support and encourage future visits to your food truck. Share highlights from the event and any special promotions or upcoming appearances to maintain momentum and keep your audience engaged.

5. Measure Success and Iterate

Finally, it's essential to measure the success of your event marketing efforts and iterate based on feedback and insights gained. Track key metrics such as foot traffic, sales, social media engagement, and customer feedback to evaluate the impact of each event and identify areas for improvement. Use this data to refine your event marketing strategy, optimize future participation, and continue driving growth for your food truck business.

Conclusion

Event marketing and collaborations are powerful strategies for food truck businesses to increase visibility, attract new customers, and generate excitement around their brand. By identifying relevant events, planning your participation effectively, collaborating with other businesses, and amplifying your presence before, during, and after the event, you can maximize the impact of your event marketing efforts and drive business growth. Drawing from personal experiences and industry best practices, you can develop a comprehensive event marketing strategy that enhances your food truck's reputation and establishes it as a beloved culinary destination in your community.

CHAPTER 7:
OPERATIONS AND LOGISTICS

Operating a food truck involves managing various logistical challenges to ensure smooth day-to-day operations and deliver exceptional customer experiences. In this chapter, we'll explore key aspects of food truck operations and logistics, drawing from personal experiences and industry best practices to help you navigate the complexities of running a successful food truck business.

1. Vehicle Maintenance and Upkeep

Maintaining your food truck in top condition is essential for ensuring safe and reliable operation. Regular vehicle maintenance helps prevent breakdowns and ensures that your truck meets health and safety standards. Here's what to consider:

- Scheduled Maintenance: Develop a maintenance schedule for routine tasks such as oil changes, tire rotations, and brake inspections. Stick to the schedule to prevent costly repairs and keep your truck running smoothly.

- Emergency Preparedness: Equip your food truck with essential tools and spare parts for quick fixes in case of emergencies. Train your staff on basic troubleshooting techniques to address common issues on the go.

- Health and Safety Compliance: Ensure that your food truck meets health and safety regulations, including cleanliness standards, proper food storage, and temperature control. Regular inspections and compliance checks help mitigate risks and protect your customers and business reputation.

2. Supply Chain Management

Efficient supply chain management is critical for maintaining adequate inventory levels and ensuring seamless operations. Here's how to efficiently manage your supply chain:

- Inventory Tracking: Implement inventory tracking systems to monitor stock levels, track usage patterns, and identify reorder points. Use technology such as point-of-sale (POS) systems or inventory management software to streamline inventory management processes.

- Vendor Relationships: Build strong relationships with suppliers and vendors to secure favorable pricing, negotiate discounts, and ensure timely deliveries. Communicate your needs and expectations clearly to vendors and address any issues promptly to maintain a reliable supply chain.

- Forecasting and Planning: Use historical sales data and market trends to forecast demand and plan inventory purchases accordingly. Anticipate seasonal fluctuations, special events, and promotional activities to avoid stockouts or excess inventory.

3. Staffing and Training

Your staff plays a crucial role in delivering exceptional customer service and maintaining operational efficiency. Here's how to manage your staffing needs effectively:

- Recruitment and Hiring: Recruit reliable and qualified staff members who are passionate about food and customer service. To make sure the candidate is a suitable fit for your team, do in-depth interviews and background checks.

- Training and Development: Provide comprehensive training to your staff on food preparation, safety protocols, customer interactions, and operational procedures. Invest in ongoing training and development to empower your team members and enhance their skills and job satisfaction.

- Scheduling and Management: Develop efficient scheduling practices to optimize staffing levels and minimize labor costs. Consider factors such as peak hours, seasonal fluctuations, and employee availability when creating schedules. Use scheduling software or apps to streamline scheduling processes and manage employee shifts effectively.

4. Route Planning and Location Selection

Choosing the right locations and routes is essential for maximizing your food truck's visibility and attracting customers. Here's how to plan your routes and select strategic locations:

- Market Research: Conduct market research to identify high-traffic areas, popular events, and target demographics in your area. Use demographic data, foot traffic patterns, and competitor analysis to inform your location selection.

- Event Participation: Participate in food truck rallies, festivals, and events to reach a broader audience and generate buzz around your brand. Research event calendars and secure spots in advance to ensure your truck's presence at popular events.

- Route Optimization: Plan your routes strategically to cover multiple locations efficiently and minimize downtime between stops. Consider factors such as traffic patterns, parking availability, and customer density when planning your route.

Personal Experience:

In my food truck business, operations and logistics were critical components of our success. We prioritized vehicle maintenance to ensure the reliability of our truck and invested in regular inspections and repairs to keep it in top condition. Supply chain management was another area of focus, and we developed strong relationships with local suppliers to ensure consistent access to high-quality ingredients. Staffing and training were also priorities, and we provided comprehensive training to our team members to deliver exceptional customer service and maintain operational efficiency. Finally, we carefully planned our routes and selected strategic locations to maximize our visibility and attract customers.

Conclusion

Effective operations and logistics are essential for running a successful food truck business. By prioritizing vehicle maintenance, managing your supply chain efficiently, investing in staff training and development, and planning your routes and locations strategically, you can optimize your operations and deliver exceptional experiences to your customers. Drawing from personal experiences and industry best practices, you can navigate the complexities of food truck operations and logistics and position your business for long-term success in the competitive culinary market.

7.1 PLANNING YOUR ROUTE AND SCHEDULE

Planning your route and schedule is a crucial aspect of food truck operations that directly impacts your visibility, customer reach, and overall profitability. In this section, we'll explore practical strategies for efficiently planning your route and schedule to maximize your food truck's success.

1. Conduct Market Research

Before planning your route and schedule, it's essential to conduct thorough market research to identify high-traffic areas, target demographics, and popular events in your area. This is the proper way to carry out market research:

- Demographic Analysis: Identify key demographic factors such as age, income level, and lifestyle preferences of your target customers. Use demographic data to inform your location selection and tailor your menu offerings to meet customer preferences.

- Foot Traffic Patterns: Analyze foot traffic patterns in different areas of your city or town to identify bustling commercial districts, popular tourist attractions, and residential neighborhoods with high pedestrian activity. Choose locations with high foot traffic to maximize visibility and attract customers.

- Competitor Analysis: Research your competitors' locations and strategies to identify gaps in the market and opportunities for differentiation. Avoid direct competition by selecting locations where your food truck can stand out and attract customers seeking unique dining experiences.

2. Identify Strategic Locations

Once you've conducted market research, it's time to identify strategic locations for your food truck. When choosing a place, keep the following things in mind:

- Visibility: Choose locations with high visibility and easy access for customers. Opt for busy street corners, popular shopping centers, or office complexes with heavy foot traffic to maximize exposure and attract attention to your food truck.

- Parking Availability: Ensure that your chosen locations have adequate parking facilities for your food truck and customers. Avoid areas with limited parking or strict parking regulations that may hinder your operations and inconvenience customers.

- Customer Density: Target areas with a high concentration of potential customers, such as business districts during lunch hours, entertainment districts on weekends, or residential neighborhoods during evenings. Consider factors such as population density, nearby attractions, and local events when selecting locations.

3. Plan Your Route Efficiently

Once you've identified strategic locations, it's time to plan your route efficiently to cover multiple locations and maximize your customer reach. Here's how to plan your route effectively:

- Use Mapping Tools: Leverage mapping tools such as Google Maps or Waze to plot your locations and plan the most efficient route. Input addresses of your chosen locations and optimize the route to minimize driving time and fuel costs.

- Consider Traffic Patterns: Take into account traffic patterns, road closures, and construction zones when planning your route. Avoid congested areas or peak traffic hours to minimize delays and ensure timely arrival at each location.

- Schedule Breaks: Factor in breaks and rest stops between locations to allow time for restocking inventory, refueling, and restroom breaks for your staff. Plan your route in a way that balances operational efficiency with adequate breaks to maintain staff morale and productivity.

4. Establish a Flexible Schedule

While it's essential to have a structured schedule, it's also important to remain flexible and adaptable to changes in customer demand, weather conditions, and unforeseen circumstances. Here's how to establish a flexible schedule:

- Monitor Customer Demand: Pay attention to customer demand and feedback to identify peak hours and popular locations. Adjust your schedule accordingly to prioritize high-demand locations during peak times and optimize your revenue potential.

- Stay Informed: Stay informed about local events, festivals, and market trends that may impact customer traffic and demand for your food truck. Capitalize on opportunities to participate in special events or collaborate with local businesses to boost your visibility and sales.

- Communicate with Customers: Keep your customers informed about your schedule and location updates through social media, email newsletters, or your website. Provide real-time updates on any changes or cancellations to ensure a positive customer experience and minimize frustration.

5. Evaluate and Iterate

Regularly evaluate the performance of your route and schedule to identify areas for improvement and optimize your operations. Monitor key metrics such as sales, customer traffic, and feedback to gauge the effectiveness of your route and schedule. Use data-driven insights to make informed decisions and iterate on your route planning strategy to maximize your food truck's success.

Conclusion

Planning your route and schedule is a critical component of food truck operations that requires careful consideration and strategic decision-making. By conducting market research, identifying strategic locations, planning your route efficiently, establishing a flexible schedule, and evaluating performance regularly, you can optimize your food truck's visibility, customer reach, and profitability. Drawing from industry best practices and personal experiences, you can develop a route and schedule planning strategy that positions your food truck for long-term success in the competitive culinary market.

7.2 MANAGING STAFF AND TRAINING

Managing staff effectively and providing comprehensive training is essential for ensuring the smooth operation of your food truck and delivering exceptional customer service. In this section, we'll explore practical strategies for managing staff and providing training that empowers your team to excel in their roles.

1. Recruitment and Hiring

Finding the right team members is the first step in building a successful food truck operation. Here's how to recruit and hire staff effectively:

- Define Job Roles: Clearly define job roles and responsibilities for each position on your food truck, including cooks, servers, cashiers, and drivers. Identify the specific skills and qualifications required for each role to attract suitable candidates.

- Advertise Job Openings: Advertise job openings through online job boards, social media, local newspapers, and community bulletin boards. Use targeted language and imagery to attract candidates who are passionate about food and customer service.

- Conduct Interviews: Conduct thorough interviews with candidates to assess their skills, experience, and fit for your team. Ask open-ended questions to gauge their communication skills, problem-solving abilities, and enthusiasm for the role.

- Check References: Verify candidates' work history and qualifications by checking references from previous employers or colleagues. Contact references directly to obtain feedback on candidates' performance, reliability, and professionalism.

2. Training and Onboarding

Once you've hired your team members, it's essential to provide comprehensive training and onboarding to set them up for success. Here's how to approach training and onboarding effectively:

- Develop Training Materials: Create training materials and resources, including manuals, handbooks, and video tutorials, to guide new hires through their roles and responsibilities. Cover topics such as food preparation, safety protocols, customer service standards, and cash handling procedures.

- Hands-On Training: Provide hands-on training opportunities for new hires to practice their skills in a real-world setting. Pair new employees with experienced team members who can mentor them and provide guidance as they learn the ropes.

- Safety Training: Prioritize safety training to ensure that all staff members understand and adhere to food safety regulations, hygiene practices, and emergency procedures. Conduct regular safety drills and refreshers to reinforce safety protocols and minimize risks.

- Customer Service Training: Emphasize the importance of excellent customer service and teach your staff how to interact with customers professionally, handle complaints effectively, and exceed customer expectations. Role-play scenarios and provide feedback to help staff members develop their customer service skills.

3. Ongoing Development

Training and development should be an ongoing process to support staff growth and continuous improvement. Here's how to foster ongoing development among your team members:

- Offer Opportunities for Advancement: Create opportunities for career advancement and growth within your food truck operation. Offer training programs, certifications, and incentives for staff members who demonstrate initiative and excel in their roles.

- Encourage Feedback: Foster a culture of open communication and feedback where staff members feel comfortable sharing their ideas, concerns, and suggestions for improvement. Actively seek feedback from your team and implement changes based on their input to enhance operations and morale.

- Invest in Education: Invest in continuing education and professional development opportunities for your staff, such as workshops, seminars, and online courses. Encourage staff members to expand their skills and knowledge in areas relevant to their roles, such as culinary techniques, food safety, or customer service.

4. Schedule Management

Efficient schedule management is essential for optimizing staffing levels and ensuring smooth operations on your food truck. Here's how to manage schedules effectively:

- Create Clear Schedules: Develop clear and concise schedules that outline staff shifts, break times, and responsibilities. Ensure that schedules are communicated to staff well in advance to allow for proper planning and coordination.

- Consider Staff Availability: Take into account staff availability, preferences, and time-off requests when creating schedules. Use scheduling software or apps to streamline scheduling processes and minimize scheduling conflicts.

- Monitor Staff Performance: Monitor staff performance and attendance regularly to identify any issues or areas for improvement. Provide constructive feedback and support to help staff members meet performance expectations and address any performance issues promptly.

5. Foster a Positive Work Environment

Creating a positive work environment is essential for fostering teamwork, morale, and employee satisfaction. Here's how to cultivate a positive work environment on your food truck:

- Lead by Example: Lead by example and demonstrate professionalism, positivity, and respect for your team members. Show appreciation for their hard work and contributions to the success of the food truck operation.

- Encourage Collaboration: Encourage collaboration and teamwork among your staff members by promoting open communication, sharing responsibilities, and celebrating successes as a team.

- Provide Recognition: Recognize and reward staff members for their achievements, whether it's exceeding sales targets, delivering exceptional customer service, or going above and beyond their duties. Provide verbal praise, incentives, or employee recognition programs to show appreciation for their efforts.

- Address Issues Promptly: Address any conflicts or issues in the workplace promptly and professionally. Listen to your team members' concerns and work together to find solutions that promote a positive and respectful work environment.

By implementing these strategies for managing staff and providing training, you can build a strong and cohesive team that contributes to the overall success of your food truck business. Investing in your team's development and well-being will not only improve employee satisfaction but also enhance the customer experience and drive business growth.

7.3 EQUIPMENT MAINTENANCE AND UPKEEP

Maintaining your food truck equipment is essential for ensuring smooth operations, food safety, and customer satisfaction. In this section, we'll delve into practical strategies for effectively managing equipment maintenance and upkeep to keep your food truck running at its best.

1. Establish a Maintenance Schedule

Creating a maintenance schedule is the first step in ensuring the proper upkeep of your food truck equipment. Here's how to set up a maintenance schedule that works:

- Routine Checks: Conduct routine checks of all equipment to identify any signs of wear and tear, damage, or malfunction. This includes kitchen appliances, refrigeration units, generators, and plumbing systems.

- Regular Servicing: Schedule regular servicing and maintenance for critical equipment components, such as HVAC systems, refrigeration compressors, and cooking appliances. Follow manufacturer recommendations for service intervals and procedures to maintain equipment warranties and ensure optimal performance.

- Document Maintenance Procedures: Document maintenance procedures and schedules for each piece of equipment to ensure consistency and accountability. Assign specific tasks to designated staff members and keep detailed records of maintenance activities, including dates, findings, and any repairs or replacements performed.

2. Conduct Preventive Maintenance

Preventive maintenance is key to extending the lifespan of your equipment and minimizing costly repairs. Here's how to implement preventive maintenance practices:

- Cleanliness* Keep equipment clean and free of debris, grease, and food residue to prevent buildup and corrosion. Establish cleaning protocols for each piece of equipment and train staff on proper cleaning techniques and frequency.

- Lubrication: Lubricate moving parts and components regularly to reduce friction and wear. Use food-grade lubricants as recommended by equipment manufacturers and follow lubrication schedules to ensure smooth operation and prevent breakdowns.

- Tighten Fasteners: Check and tighten loose fasteners, bolts, and screws on equipment regularly to prevent vibration-related damage and ensure stability and safety. Use appropriate tools and torque specifications to avoid over-tightening or stripping threads.

3. Address Repairs Promptly

Addressing equipment repairs promptly is crucial for preventing downtime and maintaining operational efficiency. Here's how to manage equipment repairs effectively:

- Diagnostic Checks: Conduct diagnostic checks and troubleshooting procedures to identify the root cause of equipment issues before attempting repairs. Consult equipment manuals, technical documentation, and online resources for guidance on diagnosing common problems and solutions.

- Prioritize Critical Issues: Prioritize repairs based on the severity of equipment issues and their impact on food quality, safety, and customer service. Address critical issues such as refrigeration failures, gas leaks, or electrical faults immediately to minimize disruptions to your operations.

- Work with Qualified Technicians: For complex repairs or specialized equipment, work with qualified technicians or service professionals who have experience and expertise in servicing food truck equipment. Research reputable service providers and establish relationships with trusted vendors for reliable support when needed.

4. Invest in Quality Equipment

Investing in quality equipment from reputable manufacturers is essential for minimizing maintenance requirements and ensuring long-term reliability. Here's how to choose and maintain quality equipment:

- Research and Compare: Research equipment options and compare features, specifications, and reviews from multiple suppliers before making purchasing decisions. Consider factors such as durability, energy efficiency, warranty coverage, and serviceability when evaluating equipment options.

- Follow Installation Guidelines: Follow manufacturer guidelines and specifications for proper installation of equipment to ensure optimal performance and safety. Hire qualified professionals to install equipment according to industry standards and local regulations.

- Register Warranties: Register equipment warranties and maintain records of purchase receipts, warranties, and service agreements for all equipment. Keep track of warranty expiration dates and renewal options to take advantage of warranty coverage and support services as needed.

5. Train Staff on Equipment Use and Care

Proper training of your staff on equipment use and care is essential for preventing accidents, injuries, and equipment damage. Here's how to train your staff effectively:

- Training Programs: Develop comprehensive training programs for new hires and existing staff members on the proper use, operation, and maintenance of all equipment in your food truck. Cover safety protocols, operating procedures, troubleshooting techniques, and emergency response procedures.

- Hands-On Practice: Provide hands-on training opportunities for staff to practice using equipment under supervision. Offer demonstrations, simulations, and role-playing exercises to reinforce learning and build confidence in handling equipment effectively.

- Safety Awareness: Emphasize the importance of safety awareness and risk mitigation when working with equipment. Teach staff how to identify potential hazards, use safety features and personal protective equipment (PPE), and respond to emergencies safely.

Conclusion

Effective equipment maintenance and upkeep are critical for ensuring the safety, efficiency, and success of your food truck operations. By establishing a maintenance schedule, conducting preventive maintenance, addressing repairs promptly, investing in quality equipment, and training staff on equipment use and care, you can minimize downtime, maximize equipment lifespan, and deliver exceptional customer experiences. Implementing these strategies will help you maintain a competitive edge in the dynamic food truck industry and position your business for long-term success.

7.4 STREAMLINING OPERATIONS FOR EFFICIENCY

Efficiency is the cornerstone of a successful food truck business. By streamlining your operations, you can maximize productivity, minimize waste, and deliver an exceptional customer experience. In this section, we'll explore practical strategies for optimizing your food truck operations for efficiency.

1. Standardize Processes and Procedures

Standardizing processes and procedures is essential for ensuring consistency and efficiency in your food truck operations. Here's how to establish standardized workflows:

- Menu Standardization: Streamline your menu by focusing on a core selection of dishes that are easy to prepare and assemble. This reduces complexity in the kitchen and allows for faster service during peak hours.

- Ordering Process: Implement a standardized ordering process to streamline customer interactions and minimize wait times. Use a clear and intuitive ordering system, whether it's a traditional cash register, tablet-based POS system, or mobile app.

- Food Preparation: Develop standardized recipes and cooking techniques to ensure consistency in food quality and portion sizes. Train your kitchen staff to follow these recipes meticulously to minimize errors and waste.

- Cleaning and Maintenance: Establish regular cleaning and maintenance schedules for your equipment, workspace, and vehicle. Assign specific tasks to team members and provide them with the necessary tools and resources to complete their duties efficiently.

2. Invest in Technology

Embracing technology can significantly enhance the efficiency of your food truck operations. Here are some technology solutions to consider:

- Point of Sale (POS) Systems: Invest in a POS system that is tailored to the needs of food trucks. Look for features such as order customization, inventory management, and integration with payment processors to streamline transactions and track sales data.

- Mobile Ordering Apps: Develop a mobile ordering app or partner with existing delivery platforms to allow customers to place orders in advance and skip the line. This lowers wait times and raises client satisfaction levels generally.

- Inventory Management Software: Use inventory management software to track ingredient usage, monitor stock levels, and automate reordering processes. This helps prevent shortages and overstocking while minimizing food waste.

- GPS Tracking: Implement GPS tracking technology to monitor the location of your food truck in real-time and optimize your route planning. This allows you to identify high-traffic areas and strategically position your truck for maximum visibility and sales.

3. Optimize Workflow

Efficient workflow is critical for maximizing throughput and minimizing bottlenecks in your food truck operation. Here's how to optimize your workflow:

- Kitchen Layout: Design your kitchen layout to facilitate a smooth flow of food preparation from station to station. Organize ingredients, utensils, and equipment in a logical sequence to minimize movement and reduce prep time.

- Staff Responsibilities: Clearly define roles and responsibilities for each member of your team to avoid confusion and overlapping tasks. Cross-train staff members so they can assist each other during peak periods and cover for absences.

- Batch Cooking: Implement batch cooking techniques to prepare large quantities of food in advance and reduce cooking time during service. This allows you to serve customers more quickly without compromising on food quality.

- Just-in-Time Inventory: Adopt a just-in-time inventory management approach to minimize food waste and storage costs. Order ingredients and supplies as needed to fulfill customer orders, rather than stockpiling excess inventory.

4. Monitor Performance and Make Adjustments

Regularly monitoring performance metrics is essential for identifying areas of improvement and making data-driven decisions. Here's how to track and analyze key performance indicators (KPIs):

- Sales Data: Analyze sales data to identify popular menu items, peak sales periods, and trends in customer preferences. Use this information to optimize your menu offerings and adjust pricing strategies accordingly.

- Customer Feedback: Solicit feedback from customers through surveys, comment cards, or online reviews to gain insights into their experience with your food truck. Pay attention to recurring complaints or suggestions and take action to address them proactively.

- Staff Productivity: Monitor staff productivity metrics such as order processing times, customer wait times, and transaction volumes. Identify opportunities to improve efficiency through additional training, process improvements, or staffing adjustments.

- Cost Management: Keep a close eye on your operating expenses, including food costs, labor costs, and overhead expenses. Look for ways to reduce waste, streamline operations, and negotiate better terms with suppliers to improve profitability.

5. Continuous Improvement

Finally, embrace a culture of continuous improvement within your food truck business. Encourage your team to suggest ideas for efficiency gains and be open to experimenting with new processes and technologies.

By implementing these strategies for streamlining your food truck operations, you can increase efficiency, reduce costs, and ultimately, drive greater success for your business. Continuously evaluate and refine your processes to stay ahead of the competition and deliver exceptional value to your customers.

CHAPTER 8:
GROWTH AND EXPANSION OPPORTUNITIES

Congratulations on successfully establishing your food truck business! As you continue on your entrepreneurial journey, it's natural to explore opportunities for growth and expansion. In this chapter, we'll explore various strategies and considerations to help you scale your food truck business effectively.

1. Assess Current Performance

Before embarking on any growth initiatives, it's essential to assess the current performance of your food truck business. Review key performance indicators such as sales revenue, customer satisfaction, and profitability to gain insights into your business's strengths and areas for improvement. This analysis will help you identify opportunities for growth and prioritize initiatives that align with your goals.

2. Expand Your Menu

One way to attract new customers and increase sales is by expanding your menu offerings. Consider introducing new dishes or seasonal specials that cater to different tastes and dietary preferences. Conduct market research to identify popular food trends and customer preferences, and tailor your menu accordingly. Be sure to maintain the quality and consistency of your offerings to keep customers coming back for more.

3. Explore Catering and Events

Catering events and private parties can be lucrative opportunities for expanding your food truck business. Reach out to event planners, businesses, and organizations in your area to offer your services for weddings, corporate events, festivals, and other special occasions. Develop customizable catering packages and promotional materials to showcase your offerings and attract potential clients. Additionally, consider participating in food truck rallies and community events to increase your visibility and reach new customers.

4. Collaborate with Other Businesses

Collaborating with other businesses can provide mutually beneficial opportunities for growth and exposure. Partner with local breweries, wineries, or coffee shops to offer food and beverage pairings or joint promotions. Explore cross-promotion opportunities with complementary businesses such as food delivery services, food bloggers, or lifestyle influencers. By leveraging each other's networks and customer bases, you can expand your reach and attract new customers.

5. Consider a Second Truck or Location

If your food truck business is thriving and you're looking to scale further, consider investing in a second truck or expanding to a brick-and-mortar location. Conduct market research to identify underserved areas or high-traffic locations where you can establish a presence. Evaluate the feasibility of expansion based on factors such as market demand, competition, and operational capacity. Secure financing if necessary and develop a detailed business plan to guide your expansion efforts.

6. Invest in Marketing and Branding

Effective marketing and branding are essential for attracting customers and differentiating your food truck business from competitors. Invest in professional branding materials such as logo design, signage, and branded merchandise to create a memorable and cohesive brand identity. Develop a comprehensive marketing strategy that includes digital marketing, social media promotion, email campaigns, and local advertising to reach your target audience effectively. Engage with your customers online, solicit feedback, and respond to reviews to build trust and loyalty.

7. Focus on Operational Efficiency

As you grow your food truck business, it's crucial to maintain operational efficiency to sustain profitability and customer satisfaction. Continuously evaluate and optimize your workflows, inventory management processes, and staffing levels to minimize waste and maximize productivity. Invest in technology solutions such as point-of-sale systems, inventory management software, and scheduling tools to streamline operations and reduce administrative burdens. Examine your spending on a regular basis and search for ways to reduce costs without sacrificing quality or service.

8. Stay Flexible and Adapt

In the dynamic and competitive food truck industry, it's essential to stay flexible and adapt to changing market conditions and consumer preferences. Monitor industry trends, competitor activities, and customer feedback to identify emerging opportunities and potential threats. Be willing to experiment with new menu items, marketing strategies, and business models to stay relevant and meet evolving customer needs. By staying agile and responsive, you can position your food truck business for long-term success and sustainable growth.

Conclusion

Growth and expansion present exciting opportunities for your food truck business to reach new heights and achieve greater success. By assessing your current performance, expanding your menu offerings, exploring catering and events, collaborating with other businesses, considering a second truck or location, investing in marketing and branding, focusing on operational efficiency, and staying flexible and adapt, you can position your business for continued growth and profitability. Remember to stay true to your brand identity and values as you pursue new opportunities, and always prioritize delivering exceptional experiences to your customers. With dedication, creativity, and strategic planning, the sky's the limit for your food truck business!

8.1 SCALING YOUR FOOD TRUCK BUSINESS

Scaling your food truck business involves expanding its reach, increasing revenue, and improving efficiency to accommodate growth. This chapter explores actionable strategies for scaling your food truck business effectively.

Assess Your Current Operations

Before scaling your food truck business, it's crucial to evaluate your current operations and identify areas for improvement. Review your sales data, customer feedback, and operational processes to gain insights into your business's strengths and weaknesses. Determine inefficiencies, bottlenecks, and expansion prospects.

1. Standardize Processes

Standardizing processes is essential for maintaining consistency and efficiency as your business grows. Document standard operating procedures (SOPs) for food preparation, customer service, inventory management, and vehicle maintenance. Train your team on these procedures to ensure everyone is on the same page and can perform their roles effectively.

2. Invest in Technology

Investing in technology can streamline your operations and improve productivity. Consider implementing a point-of-sale (POS) system to manage transactions, track sales data, and streamline inventory management. Utilize scheduling software to optimize staffing levels and manage employee schedules efficiently. Explore mobile ordering apps to provide convenience to customers and reduce wait times.

3. Expand Your Menu Strategically

Expanding your menu can attract new customers and increase revenue, but it's essential to do so strategically. Analyze customer preferences, market trends, and competitor offerings to identify menu items with high demand. Introduce new dishes gradually and monitor their performance to ensure they resonate with your target audience. Maintain a balance between innovation and consistency to keep customers satisfied.

4. Explore Additional Revenue Streams

Diversifying your revenue streams can help stabilize your income and mitigate risks associated with seasonal fluctuations or unforeseen events. Consider offering catering services for events, weddings, and corporate functions. Explore partnerships with local businesses for cross-promotion opportunities. Sell branded merchandise such as t-shirts, hats, or mugs to generate additional income and promote your brand.

5. Expand Your Reach

Expanding your reach beyond your current location can help you tap into new markets and attract a broader customer base. Explore opportunities to participate in festivals, farmers markets, and community events in neighboring areas. Consider partnering with local businesses to host pop-up events or collaborate on promotional campaigns. Leverage social media and digital marketing to raise awareness of your food truck and attract customers from different locations.

6. Increase Operational Efficiency

Improving operational efficiency is crucial for scaling your food truck business sustainably. Analyze your workflow and identify areas where you can streamline processes, reduce waste, and optimize resource allocation. Invest in training for your team to enhance their skills and productivity. Regularly review your expenses and look for opportunities to cut costs without sacrificing quality or service.

7. Build a Strong Brand

Building a strong brand identity is essential for standing out in a competitive market and attracting loyal customers. Develop a unique brand personality that resonates with your target audience and reflects your values and mission. Invest in professional branding materials such as logo design, signage, and packaging to create a memorable and cohesive brand experience. Engage with your audience on social media, respond to customer feedback, and foster a sense of community around your brand.

Conclusion

Scaling your food truck business requires careful planning, strategic decision-making, and a commitment to continuous improvement. By standardizing processes, investing in technology, expanding your menu strategically, exploring additional revenue streams, expanding your reach, increasing operational efficiency, and building a strong brand, you can scale your business effectively while maintaining the quality of your offerings and the satisfaction of your customers. Keep an eye on market trends, listen to feedback from your customers, and be prepared to adapt your strategies as needed to ensure long-term success and sustainability. With dedication and perseverance, you can take your food truck business to new heights of growth and profitability.

8.2 DIVERSIFYING REVENUE STREAMS

Diversifying revenue streams is a crucial strategy for food truck businesses looking to increase income, minimize risk, and capitalize on opportunities for growth. In this chapter, we'll explore actionable ways to diversify your revenue streams effectively.

1. Catering Services

One of the most lucrative revenue streams for food truck businesses is catering services. Catering allows you to serve large groups of people at events such as weddings, corporate functions, and private parties. To start offering catering services, you'll need to:

- Develop a catering menu: Create a specialized menu tailored to catered events, featuring popular dishes from your food truck menu as well as customizable options.
- Invest in catering equipment: Purchase or rent equipment such as chafing dishes, serving trays, and utensils to facilitate on-site food service at events.
- Market your catering services: Promote your catering services through your website, social media channels, and networking events. Reach out to event planners, wedding venues, and corporate clients to pitch your services and secure bookings.

2. Wholesale and Retail Sales

Another way to diversify your revenue streams is by selling your products wholesale to other businesses or retail to consumers. Consider the following strategies:

- Wholesale partnerships: Partner with local cafes, grocery stores, or specialty shops to sell your food truck's products on a wholesale basis. Package your items in bulk and offer competitive pricing to attract wholesale buyers.
- Retail opportunities: Explore opportunities to sell your branded merchandise, such as t-shirts, hats, or tote bags, to customers directly. Set up an online store or sell your merchandise at local markets, festivals, and events to generate additional income and promote your brand.

3. Food Truck Franchising

If your food truck business has proven successful and you're looking to expand further, consider franchising your concept to other aspiring entrepreneurs. Franchising allows you to:

- Expand your brand: Franchising enables you to grow your brand presence in new markets without the need for significant capital investment.

- Generate franchise fees and royalties: Franchisees pay upfront franchise fees and ongoing royalties in exchange for the right to operate under your brand and business model.
- Provide training and support: Offer comprehensive training and ongoing support to franchisees to ensure they adhere to your brand standards and achieve success with their businesses.

4. Online Cooking Classes and Workshops

With the increasing popularity of online learning, offering cooking classes and workshops can be a lucrative revenue stream for food truck businesses. Here's how to get started:

- Develop a curriculum: Design cooking classes or workshops based on your expertise and culinary specialties. Consider offering classes on topics such as basic cooking techniques, ethnic cuisines, or specific dishes featured on your food truck menu.
- Choose a platform: Select an online platform to host your classes, such as Zoom, Google Meet, or a dedicated learning management system (LMS). Ensure the platform offers features such as live streaming, screen sharing, and interactive Q&A sessions.
- Market your classes: Promote your cooking classes through your website, social media channels, and

email newsletters. Partner with influencers or food bloggers to reach a wider audience and attract participants to your classes.

5. Mobile App Development

Developing a mobile app for your food truck business can open up new revenue streams and enhance the customer experience. Consider the following opportunities:

- Online ordering and delivery: Implement a mobile ordering and delivery system within your app to allow customers to place orders for pickup or delivery directly from their smartphones.
- Loyalty program: Create a loyalty program within your app to reward frequent customers with discounts, special offers, and exclusive perks. Encourage repeat business and customer loyalty through personalized incentives and rewards.
- In-app advertising: Monetize your app by incorporating targeted advertising from local businesses or complementary brands. Generate additional revenue through sponsored content, banner ads, or in-app promotions.

6. Merchandising and Brand Partnerships

Selling branded merchandise and forming partnerships with other brands can diversify your revenue streams and increase brand visibility. Consider the following strategies:

- Branded merchandise: Develop a line of branded merchandise such as t-shirts, hats, stickers, or reusable water bottles featuring your food truck's logo and branding. Sell these items at your food truck, online store, or local markets to generate additional income and promote brand awareness.
- Brand partnerships: Collaborate with other brands or businesses to create co-branded products or experiences. For example, partner with a local brewery to create a signature beer pairing menu or collaborate with a dessert shop to offer exclusive dessert options at your food truck.

Conclusion

Diversifying revenue streams is essential for food truck businesses looking to increase income, minimize risk, and capitalize on growth opportunities. By exploring catering services, wholesale and retail sales, food truck franchising, online cooking classes and workshops, mobile app development, merchandising, and brand partnerships, you can create multiple streams of income and build a more resilient and sustainable business model. Keep an eye on market trends, customer preferences, and emerging opportunities to identify new revenue streams and stay ahead of the competition. With creativity, innovation, and strategic planning, you can diversify your revenue streams and take your food truck business to new heights of success.

8.3 FRANCHISING OR LICENSING YOUR CONCEPT

Franchising or licensing your food truck concept can be an exciting opportunity to expand your brand presence, reach new markets, and generate additional revenue streams. In this chapter, we'll explore the steps involved in franchising or licensing your concept effectively.

1. Understand the Difference Between Franchising and Licensing

Before deciding whether to franchise or license your food truck concept, it's essential to understand the difference between the two models:

- Franchising: In a franchise model, you grant franchisees the right to use your brand name, business model, and operating systems in exchange for upfront franchise fees and ongoing royalties. Franchisees operate independently-owned businesses under your brand's umbrella and are subject to your standards and guidelines.
- Licensing: In a licensing model, you grant licensees the right to use your brand name and intellectual property (IP) for a specific period and within defined parameters. Licensees pay licensing fees or royalties for the use of your brand, but they retain more

control over their operations compared to franchisees.

Decide which model aligns best with your goals, resources, and growth strategy.

2. Develop a Solid Business Model

Before franchising or licensing your food truck concept, it's crucial to have a solid and proven business model in place. Ensure that your concept is unique, scalable, and financially viable. Consider factors such as target market demographics, menu offerings, pricing strategy, and operational efficiency. Conduct market research to assess demand for your concept in potential franchise or license territories.

3. Establish Brand Standards and Guidelines

Maintaining consistency and quality across all franchise or license locations is essential for protecting your brand reputation and ensuring customer satisfaction. Develop comprehensive brand standards and operating guidelines covering areas such as:

- Menu offerings and pricing
- Food preparation and presentation
- Customer service standards

- Brand messaging and marketing materials
- Operational procedures and best practices

Provide thorough training and ongoing support to franchisees or licensees to help them adhere to your brand standards effectively.

4. Create Franchise or License Agreements

Draft legally binding franchise or license agreements that outline the terms and conditions of the relationship between you and your franchisees or licensees. Work with a legal advisor experienced in franchising and licensing to ensure that your agreements comply with relevant laws and regulations. Key elements to include in your agreements may include:

- Franchise or license fees and royalties
- Territory rights and exclusivity
- The length of the contract and the opportunities for renewal
- Brand usage and intellectual property rights
- Performance expectations and quality standards
- Termination and dispute resolution procedures

5. Provide Training and Support

Offer comprehensive training programs and ongoing support to franchisees or licensees to help them succeed with their businesses. Provide initial training covering areas such as:

- Food preparation and safety
- Customer service and sales techniques
- Business operations and management
- Marketing and branding strategies

Offer ongoing support through regular communication, site visits, and access to resources such as operations manuals, training materials, and marketing collateral.

6. Market Your Franchise or License Opportunity

Promote your franchise or license opportunity to potential candidates through various channels, including:

- Your website: Create a dedicated section on your website outlining the benefits of franchising or licensing with your brand and providing information about the application process.
- Industry events and trade shows: Attend franchising and licensing expos and industry

conferences to network with potential candidates and showcase your concept.
- Franchise broker networks: Partner with reputable franchise brokers and consultants who can help match you with qualified franchisees or licensees.
- Social media and online advertising: Utilize social media platforms and targeted online advertising to raise awareness of your franchise or license opportunity and attract interested candidates.

7. Select and Vet Franchisees or Licensees Carefully

Choose franchisees or licensees who align with your brand values, have relevant experience and skills, and demonstrate a commitment to success. Develop a thorough vetting process that includes:

- Reviewing applications and conducting interviews
- Performing background checks and verifying financial stability
- Assessing suitability through personality assessments or aptitude tests
- Providing disclosure documents and financial projections

Selecting the right franchisees or licensees is crucial for the success of your expansion efforts and the long-term health of your brand.

Conclusion

Franchising or licensing your food truck concept can be a rewarding way to expand your brand presence, reach new markets, and generate additional revenue streams. By understanding the differences between franchising and licensing, developing a solid business model, establishing brand standards and guidelines, creating comprehensive franchise or license agreements, providing training and support, marketing your opportunity effectively, and selecting and vetting franchisees or licensees carefully, you can build a successful and sustainable franchise or licensing program that enhances your brand's value and accelerates your growth. With careful planning, strategic execution, and a commitment to excellence, franchising or licensing your food truck concept can open up exciting opportunities for your business and propel you to new heights of success in the competitive food industry.

8.4 EXPLORING BRICK-AND-MORTAR OPTIONS

While food trucks offer flexibility and mobility, exploring brick-and-mortar options can provide stability, increased visibility, and opportunities for growth. In this chapter, we'll delve into the considerations and steps involved in transitioning from a food truck to a brick-and-mortar establishment.

1. Assess Your Business Needs

Before making the leap to a brick-and-mortar location, it's essential to assess your business needs and goals. Consider factors such as:

- Customer demand: Evaluate whether there is sufficient demand for your offerings in a fixed location. Analyze sales data, customer feedback, and market trends to gauge potential success.
- Financial viability: Determine whether you have the financial resources to cover the costs associated with a brick-and-mortar establishment, including rent, utilities, permits, and equipment.
- Brand positioning: Consider how a brick-and-mortar location aligns with your brand identity and positioning. Ensure that the atmosphere

and experience you provide in a fixed location reflect the essence of your food truck concept.

2. Choose the Right Location

Selecting the right location for your brick-and-mortar establishment is crucial for attracting customers and driving foot traffic. When selecting a site, take into account the following aspects:

- Foot traffic and visibility: Look for high-traffic areas with plenty of pedestrian activity and visibility. Consider locations near shopping centers, office buildings, tourist attractions, or residential neighborhoods.
- Demographics: Research the demographics of the area, including income levels, age groups, and consumer preferences. Choose a location that aligns with your target market and customer base.
- Competition: Assess the competitive landscape in the area and determine whether there is room for your concept. Look for gaps in the market or opportunities to differentiate yourself from existing establishments.

3. Secure Financing

Opening a brick-and-mortar establishment requires significant upfront investment, so securing financing is essential. Explore financing options such as:

- Small business loans: Apply for a small business loan from a bank or financial institution to cover startup costs, leasehold improvements, and initial operating expenses.
- Investors: Seek investment from angel investors, venture capitalists, or private equity firms who are interested in supporting your expansion efforts in exchange for equity or a stake in your business.
- Crowdfunding: Consider launching a crowdfunding campaign on platforms like Kickstarter or Indiegogo to raise funds from supporters and backers who believe in your concept.

4. Negotiate Lease Terms

When leasing a brick-and-mortar location, negotiating favorable lease terms is critical for your long-term success. Consider the following lease terms:

- Rent: Negotiate a lease agreement with a competitive rent rate that aligns with your budget and projected revenue. Factor in annual rent increases and negotiate options for lease renewal.

- Lease duration: Determine the length of the lease term based on your business plan and growth projections. Aim for a lease term that provides stability while allowing flexibility for future expansion or relocation if needed.
- Tenant improvements: Negotiate tenant improvement allowances or concessions from the landlord to cover the costs of leasehold improvements, renovations, and upgrades to the space.

5. Design and Build Out Your Space

Designing and building out your brick-and-mortar space is an opportunity to create a welcoming and immersive experience for your customers. Consider the following steps:

- Hire a professional designer: Work with an experienced designer or architect to create a layout and design that reflects your brand identity and enhances the customer experience.
- Obtain necessary permits: Ensure that you obtain all required permits and approvals from local authorities before beginning construction or renovations. This may include building permits, health permits, zoning approvals, and liquor licenses.
- Source equipment and furnishings: Purchase or lease equipment, furniture, and fixtures for your

establishment, including kitchen equipment, seating, decor, and signage.
- Build out the space: Hire contractors and tradespeople to complete the build-out of your space according to your design specifications. Assist suppliers and vendors in coordinating the prompt delivery of supplies and equipment.

6. Develop a Marketing Plan

Once your brick-and-mortar establishment is ready to open, it's essential to develop a comprehensive marketing plan to attract customers and generate buzz. Consider the following marketing strategies:

- Grand opening event: Host a grand opening event to celebrate the launch of your brick-and-mortar location and attract attention from the local community. Offer special promotions, discounts, and giveaways to encourage attendance and generate excitement.
- Digital marketing: Utilize digital marketing channels such as social media, email marketing, and online advertising to promote your brick-and-mortar establishment and engage with potential customers. Create content that highlights your menu offerings, ambiance, and unique selling points.
- Local partnerships: Forge partnerships with local businesses, community organizations, and influencers to cross-promote your brick-and-mortar

location and reach a wider audience. Collaborate on events, promotions, and co-branded initiatives to increase visibility and drive traffic to your establishment.

7. Monitor and Adapt

Once your brick-and-mortar establishment is up and running, it's crucial to monitor performance closely and adapt your strategies as needed. Keep track of key performance indicators such as sales, customer feedback, and foot traffic to identify areas for improvement and capitalize on opportunities for growth. Stay responsive to market trends, customer preferences, and competitor actions to maintain a competitive edge and ensure the long-term success of your brick-and-mortar venture.

Conclusion

Transitioning from a food truck to a brick-and-mortar establishment presents exciting opportunities for growth and expansion. By assessing your business needs, choosing the right location, securing financing, negotiating lease terms, designing and building out your space, developing a marketing plan, and monitoring performance closely, you can successfully navigate the transition and build a thriving brick-and-mortar business that complements your food truck concept. With careful planning, strategic execution, and a commitment to delivering exceptional experiences to your customers, you can take your food business to new heights of success in the competitive restaurant industry.

CONCLUSION

In the journey of starting and running a food truck business, we've explored every aspect from understanding the industry to navigating legalities, crafting a concept, managing finances, sourcing ingredients, marketing strategies, operational logistics, and exploring growth opportunities. Through this comprehensive guide, we've aimed to equip you with the knowledge and insights needed to succeed in the dynamic and competitive world of mobile food entrepreneurship.

Starting with an understanding of the food truck phenomenon, we delved into the advantages, challenges, and market analysis, laying a solid foundation for your venture. We then moved on to crafting your food truck concept, emphasizing the importance of identifying your niche, developing a menu, ensuring food safety, and designing your truck.

In the realm of business planning and financial management, we emphasized the necessity of a robust business plan, budgeting, funding options, and pricing strategies to ensure profitability and sustainability. Understanding legal and regulatory considerations, including licensing, health regulations, insurance, and taxation, is crucial for compliance and risk management.

Sourcing ingredients and suppliers responsibly, maintaining quality and consistency, and managing inventory efficiently are essential for delivering exceptional food and customer experiences. We explored various marketing and branding strategies, including building a strong brand identity, establishing an online presence, and leveraging social media and event marketing to attract and retain customers.

In operations and logistics, we discussed planning routes and schedules, managing staff and training, maintaining equipment, and streamlining operations for efficiency. Finally, we explored growth and expansion opportunities, whether through scaling your business, diversifying revenue streams, franchising, licensing, or transitioning to a brick-and-mortar establishment.

As you embark on your food truck journey, remember that success requires dedication, hard work, and a willingness to adapt to changing circumstances. Stay true to your vision, listen to your customers, and continuously seek opportunities for improvement and innovation. With passion, perseverance, and the knowledge gained from this guide, you're well-equipped to navigate the exciting and rewarding world of food truck entrepreneurship. Bon appéti, and here's to your success!

www.ingramcontent.com/pod-product-compliance
Lightning Source LLC
Chambersburg PA
CBHW050055230526
45470CB00004B/1545